Augustus J. Thébaud, R. S. Bross

The Twit-Twats

A Christmas Allegorical Story of Birds

Augustus J. Thébaud, R. S. Bross

The Twit-Twats
A Christmas Allegorical Story of Birds

ISBN/EAN: 9783337379353

Printed in Europe, USA, Canada, Australia, Japan

Cover: Foto ©ninafisch / pixelio.de

More available books at **www.hansebooks.com**

Frolicsome Twit-Twats.

Frontispiece.

The Twit-Twats.

A Christmas Allegorical Story of Birds

CONNECTED WITH THE INTRODUCTION OF SPARROWS INTO THE

NEW WORLD.

BY

REV. AUG. J. THÉBAUD, S.J.

NEW YORK:
THE CATHOLIC PUBLICATION SOCIETY CO.,
9 BARCLAY STREET.
1881.

CONTENTS.

	PAGE
PREFACE,	5

CHAPTER I.
Preliminary, . . . 7

CHAPTER II.
Origin of the Twit-Twats, ... 12

CHAPTER III.
A Sorrowful Christmas Day, . . . 17

CHAPTER IV.
A Brief Glance at the Harmonies of Creation, ... 26

CHAPTER V.
A Description of some strange Natural Habits of the Twit-Twats considered as Types of Human Beings, ... 31

CHAPTER VI.
The Beginning of a fierce Battle between two hostile Tribes of Birds, . . 38

CHAPTER VII.
A glorious Battle-Field and the first great Twit-Twat Victory. 45

CONTENTS.

CHAPTER VIII.

Suspension of Hostilities—Mating of the Birds—Building of their Nests, . . . 52

CHAPTER IX.

Ominous Rising of a new Native Leader—Multiplication of both Races, . 62

CHAPTER X.

The Sparrows' Rustication ended by an eventful Catastrophe—Return of the Birds, . . 69

CHAPTER XI.

War again and Confusion—Final Success of the Twit-Twats, ... 81

CHAPTER XII.

Christmas again—The Winter Festival of the Sparrows, ... 88

PREFACE.

HE details of natural history contained in these pages can be thoroughly relied upon, for they have all been witnessed and carefully observed by the writer. Some of these details are generally known, others have escaped the attention of naturalists. It is to be hoped that none of them will be disdainfully set aside as far-fetched or improbable. They are all the result of strict and conscientious observation.

The inference they point out with regard to a numerous class of human beings is also—the writer hopes—perfectly natural, nay, striking. It is not given, however, as absolute truth. Still, the coincidences on both sides are so remarkable and so many that it is difficult not to admit a close connection between both. But, particularly as the book is intended for "the amusement of young and grown children," there is no great fear that criticism will be too harsh on the author, who writes throughout with the greatest simplicity and good-nature, and with a desire to please. Besides, this is not a philosophical disquisition, requiring the greatest attention to principles and conclusions, authorities and historical sources, dates, texts, learned languages, critical discussion of doubtful points, etc., etc. Consequently there will be no foot-notes, or very few. Finally, the intention is not to impose the writer's *ipse dixit* on the reader, who will suit his own taste on the subject and admit the resemblance or reject it as he likes, provided he does not impugn the writer's motives nor accuse him of deliberate untruth.

We have seen with our own eyes the sparrows establish their quarters in spite of numerous obstacles, fight with the elements, endure the hardships of winter and enjoy the sweetness of summer, visibly enter into friendship and alliance with some of their congeners, and engage in bitter strife with others of the same family. We have witnessed their fights, their conquests, their triumphs; their domestic felicity or the reverse; the subordination in their families or their contentions and feuds; the use they make of the cottages given them, or the building of their awkward nests. All these have attracted our notice, as well as their "rustication" at the end of summer and their choice of residences for our long winters. These facts and many others must be now admitted as acquired to "science," according to the usual language of the day;

and the man would be a severe critic indeed who should refuse to admit that human beings very often offer to an attentive observer the same material, social, moral phenomena. This is all we contend for; and this once admitted, the close weaving of our story must be conceded by all critics, severe or not.

The series of observations here detailed at length comprise a whole year, from Christmas, 187-, to the same epoch in 187-. The first was a hard day on the poor sparrows; the second, on the contrary, happened to be a glorious one, ending in triumph and delirious joy. If some few of our young readers, on Christmas day of this present year, are sad and dejected on account of some mishap, their courage may be supported by the example of the birds. For the greater number, however, we hope it will be a season of unalloyed contentment; and by these the whole book will be read with relish, particularly the last pages, which close on a grand tableau of frisky gambols and true merry-making. Besides, for the Christian, sadness itself becomes sweet at the sight of a new-born Saviour, for, as the French carol says:

> "Si ses doux yeux versent des pleurs,
> C'est bien pour nos péchés et non pas ses douleurs." *

Still, on His face in the crib we oftener see smiles than tears. On His Mother's knees, and with angels around, there is in His eyes such a glimpse of heaven that the heaviest misfortunes are lightened and the raging storms of human passion are calmed. He brought gentle peace to earth. Thus, for everybody the coming of Christ is the happiest as well as the holiest season of the year; and even creatures deprived of reason seem to feel it and to receive their share of simple joy and hearty pleasure at that season. No wonder that among birds particularly this should take place. They are half angels by their wings, and they fill the air with their songs, the same as cherubs and seraphs, raising their voice around the throne of God, enrapture heaven by an everlasting harmony.

> * From His soft eyes, alas! salt tears do flow,
> But our own sin, not pain of His, 'tis gives Him sorrow.

THE TWIT-TWATS.

CHAPTER I.

PRELIMINARY.

A GLANCE at some previous occurrences is necessary before our true story begins; for the Twit-Twat family could not be sufficiently known unless we went back to its progenitors. They are not natives of North America; they are adopted citizens, and their place of origin and the various circumstances of their immigration must be narrated in detail, if we wish to understand their history. The portentous Christmas day which decided their destiny on their first introduction into the city of Troy on the Hudson was not—far from it—the beginning of their existence as a race. They could claim a long line of ancestors; and to know well their aptitudes, their characteristics, what they like or dislike, their physical and moral leanings—everything, in fact, which ethnographers are very exact in giving in full when they speak of any family, tribe, or nation—something, at least, of their former life in the Old World must be hastily sketched and faithfully described, in order to render more intelligible the rather queer antics they began to play as soon as they landed on the broad expanse of the New World. In particular, why they came must be laid down first, or their subsequent history could not be at all understood.

An immense calamity threatening the splendid city of New York was the cause of their introduction into North America. People at this moment may have forgotten it. It is proper to refresh the memory of the thoughtless, for whom the greatest facts of history pass on unperceived and are buried the day after in the tomb of the Capulets.

New York is indeed a vast city, with avenues ten miles long from south to north, with cross-streets running from the East River to the broad Hudson, with stately public buildings and palatial houses rising to heaven and defying the skies. From all parts of the continent people come to live in it. At the time our story opens there were none of the elevated railroads which now transport you in a moment from the

New York Parks eaten up by Worms—Sparrows Introduced.

Battery to the Harlem River; but the streets were already crowded with horse-cars running in all directions—along the avenues, through a great number of cross-streets, following the curving line of the wharves and piers, or, in belt fashion, through the heart of the monster. As to the number of carts, wagons, carriages, vehicles of every description, who could count them? Hear the noise, listen to the public venders, to the hoarse newsboys, to the laughing urchins, to the shrill-voiced little girls, and tell me how you are pleased with such a concert! See the hurrying pedestrians on the sidewalks, cross-streets, in every possible and impossible direction. Do you find anything of the kind in Paris, in Naples, in Constantinople, in Pekin? Consider, in fine, the whole surface of Manhattan Island—which the Dutch, it is said, bought from the Indians for the mighty sum of sixteen dollars and a quarter—and inform me, if you can, of the actual value of its real estate now, if your purse were large enough to purchase the whole! But, in spite of an apparent confusion, you must admire this broad metropolis, sitting like a queen in front of an incomparable bay, and skirted right and left by two mighty streams covered with vessels from all the seaports of the world.

Nor was there, at the time our story begins, any question yet of bridging the Harlem River, or of grading the rocky surface of Westchester County for extending out there the boulevards and avenues of the city. Still, the city was already so vast that the miniature parks formerly planted to afford recreation and fresh air to the overworked citizens were now become far too small for any useful purpose, and could not, except with an evident abuse of language, be called the "lungs" of so huge a body. Central Park, therefore, had been planned, and trees and shrubs planted, ready to grow, and shoot out their leaves, and open their sweet blossoms. Eight hundred acres of ground! There surely would be shade and coolness, especially on Sunday afternoons in summer.

But the hopeful citizens saw with terror the frailty of their hopes when immense armies of ugly, slimy, ferociously active caterpillars began to swarm on all the trees planted in the streets, on all the green shrubs and herbs of the small pleasure-grounds crowded with children every afternoon. Before the end of summer all these pretended parks were generally deserted as worse for shade and coolness than the streets and dusty avenues even. The trees in Union Square had been devoured; the sycamores in Washington Square were become merely huge stumps deprived of all beauty; the young plantations in Madison Square, scarcely green the year before, seemed ready to die before autumn; and, worse than all, black battalions of the devouring hordes appeared to be already trending their way up north towards the last hope of the bewildered citizens. Central Park itself seemed to be doomed!

Then a cry of anguish issued forth from all lungs and all throats; men were ready to give up everything in despair, when certain benevolent and intelligent individuals suddenly broke out in a loud exclamation: "We must have sparrows!"

The Twit-Twat family was not comprised in the first broods brought in from

Europe, so that we have not closely to investigate the origin of these first immigrants. We doubt the truth, however, of what was generally said at the time, that they were in the bulk English, or perhaps Scotch, birds, and we may confidently declare some of our reasons, which, it is hoped, will not prove uninteresting to the reader. It is not, certainly, about the rich mansions of the West End of London that sparrows will naturally be prolific; they could scarcely find there the homely quarters where they like to nestle, and the burly London servants would never be good-natured enough to spread crumbs and seeds for them in time of scarcity. As to insects and worms in summer, the sparrow might as well look for them in the sea or on the bare rocks. The country villages, also, and the farms of plenteous England are often too prim and well kept for the rather loose habits of the sparrows, and rustic boys are too fond of catching small birds to allow them an indefinite increase. Consequently, though our eyes have never been blessed with a sight of Great Britain, it can be said with assurance that sparrows are not very common in England, at least comparatively. The same may be said to a great degree of the northern kingdom, except, perhaps, of the Highlands, which were, however, too far out of the way for the purpose in question. A large number of birds were required; Ireland, therefore, was the only place where they could be found in any quantity, chiefly the counties of Wexford and Waterford, the nearest to Great Britain, whence they could be carried by stealth to Liverpool, and there muster for English or Scotch birds, as you prefer.

Yes, all over Ireland they swarm! The country is exactly made for them. The few immense parks and rich mansions of absentee landlords they can afford to pass by; but there are numberless villages, hamlets, farm-houses just made for them; ruins with holes and cavities; trees and shrubs growing wild around the hut of the cottier, and chiefly the eaves of the thatched cottages; churches on the roofs of which they can chirp to their hearts' content; plenty of worms and insects, which, everybody knows, are their dainty tidbits and the principal food of their young. As to the people, they are just made to please the sparrows, as the sparrows are made to please them. Both people and sparrows are noisy, lively, sociable, humble in their garb, easily satisfied, enduring hardships without murmur, prolific beyond calculation, always jolly, indestructible as a race, spreading out over large continents, but unable to cross the seas unless they are carried across. Who shall say that they cannot agree together? So that you may go wherever you like in Ireland, and you will find sparrows in abundance.

When they first arrived in New York the birds were petted as they had never been before, as they never expected to be. Brightly painted little houses had been built for them, with numerous rows of nice little holes, and capacious chambers inside. These houses were placed on the tops of long poles which were set up in the various parks of the city, or they were nailed to the branches of far-spreading trees. Many a citizen hung up at least one small sparrow-cottage in the tree which tried to grow in front of his door. As to crumbs and dainty bits, there was perfect recklessness: think of pound-cake and sponge-cake, broken macaroons and marchpane! Had ever such a table been spread anywhere else before any family of the passer kind? Hence the sparrows began soon to thrive, and there was a comparative decrease in the ugly army of caterpillars.

It was among the aristocratic classes especially of the New World that these kind feelings had been manifested in favor of the little Irish strangers; and although *some* men would not have objected to receiving them from the neighborhood of Waterford as well as from that of Birmingham, still there is no doubt in our mind that there would not have been so reckless an expenditure of cake and kindness generally had the real origin of the birds been known. They profited, therefore, by the obscurity thrown purposely around the place they came from; and some rich families having fine stone-front houses on Fifth Avenue and around Stuyvesant Square, with large and handsome creepers running to the very top of the buildings and about the doors and windows, had no hesitation in placing the newly-arrived birds among the rich foliage and the entangled vegetation, there to build their nests and chirp all day long in the very iron frames of the balconies. Do you suppose, gentle reader, that many ladies would have allowed them to peep through the grating of the windows into their very rooms and boudoirs, had they known that these inquisitive little fellows were fresh from Irish cottages, and perhaps from the moors of Tipperary? Yet so it was; but at the time no one suspected it, and it was only much later on that the native country of the birds finally became known, to the disgust of many highly aristocratic families of the original Dutch or English stock, who in some instances—as we shall soon mention in detail—had to cut to the very roots of the creepers in which the most favored sparrows had nestled and multiplied.

These preliminary remarks were necessary to introduce the interesting family of which it is now proper to give a detailed account.

CHAPTER II.

ORIGIN OF THE TWIT-TWATS.

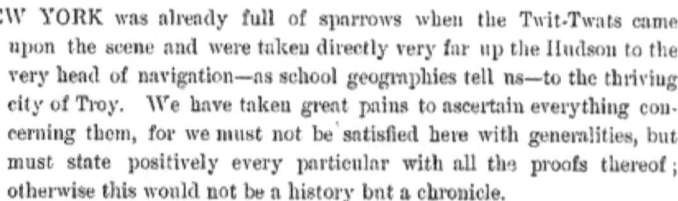

EW YORK was already full of sparrows when the Twit-Twats came upon the scene and were taken directly very far up the Hudson to the very head of navigation—as school geographies tell us—to the thriving city of Troy. We have taken great pains to ascertain everything concerning them, for we must not be satisfied here with generalities, but must state positively every particular with all the proofs thereof; otherwise this would not be a history but a chronicle.

During a residence of many years in Troy we became acquainted with an Irishman called O'Murphy—Murrogh O'Murphy: he had not dropped the O, as most of the tribe have done, we must say, reluctantly, to their disgrace. It was sufficient to look at him and talk a few moments with him to be persuaded that he belonged to the great clan of the O'Murphys, a branch of the Hy-Felimy, the nearest neighbors, in the south of Ireland, to the celebrated tribe of the Hy-Kinsellas. Murrogh O'Murphy was from the county of Wexford, of course, and had spent all his life in the suburbs of New Ross, at the confluence of the Nore and the Barrow, as his ancestors had done for many ages before him. It was he, or rather his boy William, who brought the Twit-Twats to Troy.

At the time we became acquainted with this family the birds lived in a Lombardy poplar under our windows, and we had witnessed many queer facts concerning them, which the reader will soon hear with great interest. We were, therefore, naturally very curious to know something of their previous history; and this, in substance, is what Murrogh O'Murphy related, with more details than would, perhaps, be pleasant to some of our readers, so that we shall abridge his narrative, though the main facts must be given.

From the door of the humble cottage occupied by the O'Murphys in New Ross you can yet see the high steeple of the new church erected not long ago by the good Augustinian friars, on the very site of the old convent chapel confiscated at the Reformation and turned into a Protestant parish church. The Church-of-Ireland men in New Ross, more generous than many others of the same denomination, gave it back more than fifty years ago to the original owners at a nominal rent of ten shillings, because they intended to transfer their parochial centre to a more fashionable part of the town. Thus the Augustinian friars came back into their own, and forthwith erected an edifice famous to this day, whose spire can be seen to a great distance. The foundation stone was laid in 1830 by the Very Rev. Daniel O'Connor, O.S.A., afterwards Bishop of Saldes; and the Very Rev. James Crane, O.S.A., then prior, labored hard to make the holy work a complete success in every respect. Near that new church stood, and stands probably yet, the gray ruins of an old Gothic structure surmounted by a cross which some said had belonged to the confiscated Augustinian convent, and some others—we are positively of this last opinion—thought were the remains of an old priory of the Canons Regular of St. Augustine, which, according to Allemande, was founded at Ross at a very early period, and long before the order of Augustinian *friars* was established in 1320 under Edward III. It was, therefore, an affair of ancient Ireland, and nothing else

This is all perfectly historical—mind it well—and the reader sees that we are profuse and precise in our statements. Should he wish to ascertain their accuracy he may look into the *History of the Augustinians*, by Father Herrera, a learned Spaniard; into the *Antiquities* of Ware on the reign of Edward III.; and into the details given by all accurate historians of the spoliations of Henry VIII., particularly of his dealings with the abbeys of Dunbrody, Tintern, Ferns, and the convent of Ross at the time of their suppression.

The only reason we can assign for these learned references is the necessity of precision with respect to the ancestors of the Twit-Twats. They had lived from time immemorial in the ruins of the old priory, more than a thousand years old, and young William O'Murphy, at that time a boy of ten, had frequently seen them in the mouldering walls; and he was greatly surprised—we have this from himself—when, as soon as the new church was built, a swarm of them alighted on the steeple on a certain day that he was on the lookout, and began to nestle in some holes which the masons had left, perhaps purposely for them, around the spire. There they twittered undisturbed for a good many years, and many of them, or their descendants, we are sure, twitter there at present.

The ancestors of the Twit-Twats, therefore, had inhabited the County Wexford from the very origin of *sparrowdom*. They were *twittering* along the Barrow when *Lavra-the-mariner*—we spare you the Gaelic name—the son of Olioll-Aine, came back from Gaul, and, going up the river with his *curraghs*, attacked Coffagh, the usurper of Leinster, and burned him in his palace of Dinn-Righ, a short distance from what is now Leighlinbridge.

The name of the future celebrated County Wexford was not then even known. It is of Danish origin, and one of the very few words which alone still attest in our days that the ferocious Scandinavians ever landed in Ireland. The ancient Twit-Twats, from their elevated position under the stone cross of the old Augustinian priory, witnessed, no doubt, the barbarities of the followers of Turgesius the Dane. Many of them, perhaps, were smoked out of their usual haunts along the Barrow and the Nore by the incendiary pirates. Still, their progeny again covered the whole land when Strongbow came over with his Anglo-Normans. The Twit-Twats, frightened at first by the new invaders, were at last reconciled—the unpatriotic rogues !—to the sway of the feudal barons by the refuge afforded them in the innumerable castles built on the whole surface of the island from sea to sea. Who has not seen in Europe the swarms of sparrows around those huge and frowning battlements, the only standing relics of now extinct feudalism ? Yet it must be said to the honor of these birds that they in general prefer the churches to the castles; and as the Fitzgeralds, Fitzharrises, Fitzhenrys, and Talbots, their nearest neighbors at the confluence of the Barrow and the Suir, built churches as well as castles, this may explain the real attachment that has always subsisted between the Twit-Twats and the descendants of Strongbow's followers, without any peril to their orthodoxy.

It would be too long to go through the subsequent events of this interesting history, and relate the frequent changes and sad fortunes which Protestantism brought to the birds as well as to men ; but this brings us down to the apparently forgotten thread of our history.

Murrogh O'Murphy had seen many of his personal friends depart for America, when he himself thought of emigrating to the New World. All his preparations were soon made, and he intended to go down the Barrow to Waterford, in order to take ship for Liverpool, and thence to cross the sea in a steamship for New York.

But his son William looked with regret at his friends the Twit-Twats, whom he was going to leave behind. Scarcely a day of his life had passed without thinking of them, looking at them, and speaking of them ; and it was a painful sacrifice to be reduced to a bare remembrance for the remainder of his days. He thought, indeed, of catching some few of the brood and carrying them with him ; but how was he to obtain permission from his father, who very likely would laugh at his nonsense?—when, lo and behold ! just a week before their departure a letter from a friend in New York was received, relating at length the introduction of the sparrows in the New World, not forgetting to dwell on the extravagance of some American citizens in favor of the homely birds, and hinting that a few dozens imported in a good-sized cage might go far to pay the whole expense of the voyage. William had thus a fine opportunity which he did not neglect; and he saw with pleasure that, instead of catching two or three and concealing them as best he might in a small, dark cage, he could now openly set his traps for a whole week, make prisoners of as many dozens as he had thought of individuals, and be at once the owner and custodian of a whole colony, which would certainly give him a great importance in the eyes of fellow-passengers across the ocean.

He set his traps wherever there was hope of catching sparrows ; but he chiefly kept his eyes open for two splendid birds which he had followed in all their wanderings for the two or three years before, and which for many months had been the occupants of the finest hole in the spire of the Augustinian church. The boy could tell the

The Twit-Twats in New Ross, Ireland.

cock among a thousand by its fearless daring and the black of its head with the deep red color of the upper feathers of its wings. As to the hen, poor thing! he had so often stolen her young in the steeple that she was as familiar to him as to her own mate. Sparing the reader all the ingenuity which William displayed in his dark plot, it is enough to say that he succeeded; gave them a place apart in the large cage by making a small compartment for them to dwell in; and when the boat finally dropped down the river with Murrogh O'Murphy and his son, these two remarkable birds shared the captivity of many others of far inferior note. This desolate couple are the original Twit-Twats of whom we are writing the momentous history.

New York harbor was reached without any loss of life; and as the O'Murphys were at once going up the Hudson to Troy, the precious cage was transferred to the lower deck of the steamer *Vanderbilt*, and arrived the next morning at its final destination.

CHAPTER III.

A SORROWFUL CHRISTMAS DAY.

HE citizens of Troy were then in the first flush of the sparrow-fever. Many had already obtained these highly-prized birds from New York, Albany, or Lansingburg; but such was the number calling for them that our friend William O'Murphy found no trouble in disposing of the whole brood at a price which astonished even his father. The two pets, however, were the last to be sold, and William would not consent to part with them except on the certainty of their being well treated. Of this he felt no doubt when a great family living on Washington Park, in Troy, paid royally for the handsome couple.

At first everything went on admirably. The Irish boy, who with his father soon found work in a foundry not far from the aristocratic square, often went to have a look at his pets, and he was highly pleased to remark that not only had they the liberty of the adjoining park, but they had been encouraged by the family to nestle in the intricate folds of an immense creeper covering the whole front of their house at the side of the square.

How could it be supposed that under such circumstances the race would become extinct? In fact, they multiplied prodigiously in a very short space of time, and the two genuine, original birds brought over by the O'Murphys became the patriarchs of as lively and numerous a tribe as ever were the celebrated Dal-Cassians of ancient Munster, so renowned in story and song. Two summers had sufficed for it.

Unfortunately, as the Dal-Cassians long ago met their doom, the Twit-Twats, too, in the very flush of their prosperity seemed destined to a like sad fate.

Already, a few months before, the lively interest long felt in New York for all sparrows had begun unaccountably to wane. Various reasons were assigned for it: the birds were very noisy, and Uppertendom could not peaceably slumber until eight or nine o'clock, whilst the fussy and numerous swarms were awake about the windows at four in summer. Besides, the nice little houses built for them, so bright and neat at first, were now growing dingy, and the birds not only did not keep them clean, but some of them had even been seen positively defiling them. Moreover, they were often perceived, after the passage of horses and mules, darting down from the upper stories of a splendid house and alighting in the middle of the street. Who could bear such vulgarity? Worst of all, after such unaccountable expeditions they often flew back to the balconies of the house, and, if a window happened to be open and the lady was at her toilette, they carried bad manners so far as to twitter and chatter as if their voyage to the street and its object could be thus publicly avowed with such an air of triumph! Evidently the birds were vulgar. Hence people began to speak mysteriously of their origin, and the secret finally came out—they were Irish!

The terrible news, originating in New York, did not fail to reach Troy in time, and the verdict of fashion in the metropolis was acquiesced in wherever it became known. War, therefore, was declared against sparrows in all aristocratic quarters, and if the whole brood could have been sent back to Europe, never to visit again the shores of fair America, the world of fashion would have rejoiced exceedingly; but the race had taken possession of the land and was henceforth indestructible.

The Twit-Twats, meanwhile, had to suffer. The splendid creeper-vine which had sheltered them for two full summers was mercilessly cut down, and the following Saturday afternoon, when William O'Murphy took his accustomed walk toward Washington Park, he was struck to the heart to see the former green bower of his dear sparrows now withered and lying about on the ground where it had bloomed a few days before. What had become of the birds? None could be seen in the trees even of the adjacent park; he had therefore to enquire. As he knew several female servants of the neighborhood, he soon found out all the particulars. Two or three days previously the vine had been rooted out by order of the lady of the house, and the servants had been employed the whole afternoon scaring away the birds not only from the block of buildings to which the mansion belonged, but even from the large trees of the square. All that could be said was that the birds had taken their flight down Second Street and across the Poestenkill Creek: they must be in South Troy!

South Troy is divided from the city proper by the Poestenkill Creek, a raging torrent full of foam and shapeless débris in the early spring, but requiring dams and locks in summer and autumn to show its title to the name of a real river or creek. Formerly there was between the city and the stream a large waste and marshy ground; but in course of time improvements have been decreed by the Common Council of Troy, and the streets of the former village, called South Troy, are now part and parcel of the city itself. But no aristocratic family would consent to live in the district; the houses and cottages are homely and almost without exception occupied by people of the indestructible Milesian race. The sparrows this time, left to their instinct, had well chosen their quarters, and would no doubt experience better treatment than from their former refined patrons. Only the question was rather puzzling to William O'Murphy: What had become of the original Twit-Twats? They were only two among a number, and the whole flock had gone God knew where. He made up his mind to employ the whole Sunday following—after having heard Mass, of course—in solving the problem.

By the help of friendly inhabitants he learned that, after following Second Street

The Twit-Twats in Washington Square, Troy

across the creek, the whole brood had turned to the east and had found themselves in a very grove, so thickly had the trees been planted along Third and Fourth Streets. These trees luxuriate especially around a large church in the neighborhood called St. Joseph's, and the sparrows might, perhaps, have recognized with delight something like their former haunts in New Ross. Finally, not to weary the reader with useless details, William O'Murphy found, to his intense pleasure, that the whole colony had already settled not only around the church, but chiefly in a convent of good sisters separated from the church by a street.

The cornices under the roof, and a multitude of nice little nooks surrounding a beautiful statue of St. Joseph, offered them a sure asylum from which they might expect never to be expelled again. And, to render William's joy more complete, he saw the very patriarchal Twit-Twats he was looking for; they had taken the finest hole of the whole front of the house! There they were, to be sure. He could have recognized them among a thousand; the hen, as well as the cock, in the midst of a numerous progeny. Here we must leave them for a while. Although they are not yet in the Lombardy poplar under our windows, they often, it is true, come to it, being separated from it by the distance only between two streets, and being attracted by the lofty branches of the trees which tower over both church and rectory.

In their pleasant little hole they were shaded from the western sun by a tall and handsome statue of St. Joseph holding in his arms the divine Child; and the neighbors remarked, with grateful surprise, that they were never seen to rest familiarly on the holy image, which they appeared to treat with instinctive reverence, as though they had known the sacred reality of which it was the emblem. They had acted quite differently in the iron balcony of the fine house where they had spent the first two years of their residence in Troy, as every one could perceive when the destruction of the large creeper revealed the real state of things hidden at first under green leaves and bright flowers.

Thus the old feathered couple spent the end of the summer and the greater part of the autumn in joy. But the fierce blasts of November taught them the insecurity of their position. Torrents of rain poured down at times and were soon frozen by the northwest wind. The rain dashed against the west front of the house, and at every storm filled the humble nest of the poor sparrows with ice. What would it be by the end of December? Moreover, occupying that side of the house towards the street, for which sparrows have always a great liking, the foolish birds never gave a thought to the interior of the convent, the well-kept garden behind, with its alleys and nooks where the nuns used to walk or sit, precisely on the side opposite to the public thoroughfare. Inside the convent grounds only could they receive the kindly help of the sisters in times of scarcity and starvation. The nuns knew nothing of what passed on the street, and consequently knew not the distress of the sparrows. Truly the birds' position was lamentable, though they were not yet fully aware of it; when the hard winter would come on they would find it out to their cost!

The church, looming up on the western side of the public highway, attracted them often, and thus removed them still farther from the interior of the friendly convent. They often flew over and beyond the church and chirruped in a row of Lombardy poplars planted along the western front of the rectory adjoining and to the north of it. This position would have suited them admirably; but it was already occupied by several other families of sparrows, chiefly by a single pair dwelling in one of the cells of a double house nailed by my predecessor on the tree planted just in front of my windows. None of the Twit-Twats—male or female—dared to push their pretensions so far as to take possession of the spare room left empty in the little wooden house; for of the two cells one only was occupied. They were no doubt afraid of meeting with a fierce opposition from the previous occupants, who in fact did not appear to be of an obliging disposition. Their reserved manners, staid habits, cautious if not dark demeanor, and thrifty situation indicated their origin with certainty. From the first I perceived that they were somewhat different birds.

Meanwhile the Twit-Twats paid me occasional visits, and after every storm that raged during the last of November and the beginning of the following month I usually remarked two poor forlorn sparrows squatting on the sill of one of my windows, pressing their tails and backs against the glass, and looking wistfully at the little birdhouse nailed to a branch of the tree at a few feet distance. So far they dared no more; as soon as the storm would be fully abated they would disappear and fly back over the house and the church, no doubt returning to their desolate quarters in front of St. Joseph's Convent.

But who were these strange sparrows for whom the Twit-Twats appeared to entertain feelings not only of distrust but apparently of dread? It is an interesting question, because of the important part they are to bear in this eventful history.

I have here only conjectures to guide me; yet they are strong conjectures, as the reader can judge. During the year I spent in Jersey City I had heard of a tradition prevalent among the people that European sparrows had been introduced into the State of New Jersey previous to their arrival in New York—how long previously no one could say. I have no doubt that by enquiring carefully into the traditions of New England reliable reports of the same nature would be obtained. The fact is that ever since the first planting of the English colonies in the Eastern States many men must have thought of introducing sparrows. Perhaps more than thirty years ago, I myself tried to obtain a hundred pairs of French birds, in order to naturalize them at Fordham; and I failed through the carelessness only of a steward employed on one of the French steamers, who made me fine promises which he never fulfilled. How long, therefore, this species of birds has existed in America cannot now be known. What is certain is that there are varieties among them, and consequently they must have come from different parts of the old continent. The same, therefore, is true of them as of the human races inhabiting the Atlantic seaboard, though not to the same extent: they were *all* strangers when they came; those who had arrived first may have grown to think themselves the real aborigines, and so to regard the later arrivals as intruders. The same, we know, has happened with men; among a certain number of the first colonists in the old thirteen States, for instance. They now very proudly call themselves *natives*.

However this may be, it is sure that the brood of sparrows which thrived under my windows before the arrival of the Twit-Twats presented the differences which I have mentioned; and it was clear that a conflict must ensue.

The pair residing in the little house must first have our attention. They had come just a year before the Twit-Twats appeared; and although they were evidently old birds—at least eight years old—still in the few summer months that elapsed before the Irish swarm's arrival they had, to the knowledge of my predecessor, hatched successfully and brought up at least three broods. All that young progeny was, at the time of my coming, living about the roof of our house or in the numerous trees which shed a grateful shade around, the old couple living all alone in one of the cells of the bird-cottage they had first occupied.

Impossible to say if it be the effect of prejudice, but I have always imagined that there was a great difference between them and all the Irish sparrows I have since become acquainted with. The venerable pair residing near my windows were certainly more sedate than any birds I have ever known from the Green Isle; and if their numerous offspring established around were as noisy and petulant as any Irish creatures, they seemed, to me at least, of so ferocious and overbearing a character as I have never found in their Irish congeners. At least I fancied so, and the reader will perhaps agree that the sequel of the story mournfully confirmed my judgment.

The month of December was already half gone when the weather, which had so far been at times squally, yet in general not over-harsh, suddenly became more threatening, and gave signs that we should have one of those extensive northwest storms which appear occasionally to come in a direct line from the very mouth of the Mackenzie River, or rather from Behring Strait.

It was a succession of fierce tempests rather which began toward the middle of December, and were to culminate with the eventful Christmas festival of 187-. The ground, already covered with snow, received a new supply almost every day. Fancy how hard it must soon have become for the poor Twit-Twats to keep alive in the cold and to find enough to eat. Meanwhile their enemies, the natives, did not fare much better; and this was not calculated to soften their obstreperous temper. I must say, however, that the two patriarchs, both hen and cock, continued to show their quiet and demure ways in the midst of the turbulent world around. They often came out of their cell and flew about in quest of food, and I confess I never did understand how they could succeed in finding enough to live. No naturalist has yet fully explained how so many sparrows can escape starvation during our long winters. The help they receive from people who throw crumbs before their doors or on the sills of their windows does not clear up the problem, for this very uncertain help cannot reach one-tenth of the birds. We prefer to think it is Providence. And here we are altogether serious, and must be so, since it is our divine Lord Himself who says that our Father in heaven feeds even the birds of the air. "Are not you of much more value than they?"

For my part I was delighted not only with the solution of such a mystery in the actual circumstances, but also with the peaceful behavior of the venerable *native* birds, to whom we will give that name for want of a better one. It may have been the result of age—eight years is a long period for sparrows—but it was also, very likely at least, the effect of an excellent natural disposition. They never engaged in fight, and showed the greatest good-nature not only for their rude offspring but even for the newly-arrived strangers, if they met any.

But this did not much assist the Twit-Twats, who, besides suffering from hunger, had no other place of refuge than the dismal hole exposed every day to the buffetings of the storm. How they escaped perishing has always been to me a matter of wonder. Birds that are so diminutive, whose organs must be so delicate and are almost microscopic, one would suppose would be incapable of resisting a single blast of winter; still, week after week they were night and day in the midst of perils without number.

Imagine the disconsolate pair fluttering from the top of the convent to the roof of the church, and finally trying to rest their wearied limbs on some window-sill of the parsonage, already covered with several inches of hard-pressed snow. How fiercely the storm used to rage on those roofs! With what madness it beat against chimneys and flues! Bricks even and slates were loosened and driven through the air, the fury of the wind appearing to be tenfold greater on the tops of buildings than in the desolate streets below. I remember on one occasion seeing a pair of feeble sparrows taken violently in their miserable flight by a sudden gust of the fierce wind, and flung, half-dead, against the walls of a neighboring edifice. The stranger-birds were all this time to the east of our house, and it must be certain that their position on the roof of the convent was indeed deplorable, though I could not see their hole from my window.

Meanwhile Christmas day was near, and preparations were everywhere going on among men for its worthy celebration. It is, no doubt, owing to a benevolent design of Providence that for Christians of the northern hemisphere—the immense majority of the Church's children—it falls in the midst of winter. That rude season is to some extent deprived of its harshness by the sweet and tender mysteries which always surround the Saviour's cradle. The thought that the Infant laid in a manger is the Eternal Word, who "in the beginning was with God and was God"; that, owing to His infinite love and compassion for man, "He was made flesh and dwelt among us," is enough to soften our heart and fill it with the sweetest emotions. Are not our eyes inclined to moisten when we behold Him, in the arms of His Mother, "weeping for our sins, not for His own sorrows"? His power created the universe, and He could in a moment annihilate His enemies; but He has deliberately deprived Himself of His might, and the tiny hands which He has assumed could not strike a blow. The guiltiest sinner need not fear Him, can approach Him with confidence, and lay down at

His feet the heavy burden of his iniquity. Although His tongue cannot yet speak, He seems already to utter the divine words which later came from His lips: "Come to me, all ye that labor and are heavy laden, and I will refresh you."

While the wind howls outside that grotto in Bethlehem, and the winter cold freezes those who prefer to remain without and reject the boon of a safe asylum, inside, around Mary and her Babe, the blast cannot be felt; for the Prince of Peace is there, and the atmosphere is tranquil wherever he condescends to lie. Hasten, therefore, ye poor and lowly shepherds. To you first the message has been brought by angels, and kings, too, will come, but only after you.

It is thus to the heart of the sinner and of the suffering poor that the Christmas festival speaks most eloquently. There is joy in the lowliest house, because it is precisely the most fit reproduction of the first dwelling of Christ on earth. Those of you, humble Christians, who are deprived, even on that day, of the commonest blessings of life, consider that your Master and Lord, when His Mother was refused admittance into a common inn and obliged to take refuge in an abandoned stable, was not better off than you are. If you suffer from cold, hunger, poverty, remember that this also was the grievous lot preordained by Almighty God for His Son. Rejoice, therefore, because you resemble Him most. You are His dear friends, since He treats you like Himself. Sharing now in His privations, you may share one day in His endless happiness in glory.

These high considerations, brought on by the narrative of a pair of disconsolate sparrows, may appear far-fetched to the critics. But the reader is reminded of the ultimate purpose of this little book, which is to look at human beings under the veil of a myth confined in appearance to diminutive birds. Our Lord Himself, in developing His heavenly doctrine before men, has placed under their eyes the consideration of the "birds of the air," adding only at the end, "Are not you of much more value than they?" We shall not pretend to say that the Twit-Twats had any knowledge of Christmas, or could profit in their sufferings, during that fearful winter, by the consideration of divine mysteries intended for the salvation of man only. But for all that there are harmonies between the animal creation and the far higher sphere of man, as will soon appear with the help of authorities not lower than the words of the Saviour Himself and of St. Paul. Here it must suffice to say that the culmination of all the Twit-Twats' troubles, and also their happy termination, happened just on Christmas day of 187-, and to this we return.

The tempest on that morning was more dreadful than it had been at any time during the fortnight. I was too busy in the church to pay any attention to the sparrows, and cannot say anything of their vicissitudes from "early morn" till after dinner. The first moment I could go to my room was at two o'clock P.M., and I had just half an hour to rest. The best rest for me was directly to look out for my little friends; and for a few minutes I was disappointed. Soon, however, I heard something like their usual twitter, but much more feeble than it had ever before seemed to me. They were evidently nearly exhausted by their long struggle against the elements. Their poor wings could scarcely support them in the air, exactly like those of young birds who venture for the first time out of their nest. They arrived, panting and breathless, and alighted in the most forlorn condition at the window of my room nearest to the much-coveted cottage of the old native pair. As it was now a question of life and death for them, they were evidently determined to occupy the empty room which they had already so often examined, and their mind was made up not to return to their former quarters.

Their little feet were resting on the snow which covered the sill. Their tails were pressed against the very glass, which enabled me to see them through the snow that formed a film on the panes; their heads were turned upwards, and they looked intently on the cottage in the poplar-tree, which certainly was their last resource in this their fatal day. Of the two rooms of the cottage, one, as was said before, was occupied by a pair of old birds; the other remained empty. The progeny of the ancient couple occupied all the holes and corners under the roof of the house; but none of them had, it seems, thought of settling in the apartment next to the patriarchs of the tribe. The position of the unfortunate strangers has been more than sufficiently described; we must see how stood the antagonistic element.

The Twit-Twats certainly regarded all the birds around as their enemies. They had been so often chased away by the colony settled at the top of the house that, although the birds in the cottage never flew at them, they could not but imagine they were of one mind with their turbulent offspring. At this precise moment of our story the old native cock, in spite of the tempest, was more than half-way out of his hole and looking down on the strangers—without moving, without showing any sign of anger. But from my room I could hear, although very indistinctly, the flutterings of many birds on the roof above, excited evidently by the presence of their hated visitors. A short moment was to decide the fate of the Twit-Twats, and this moment came sooner than I expected. While I was still looking at them on the window-sill they both rose suddenly and swiftly through the tempestuous air, and rested at once near the coveted entrance to the only refuge left them. The old native patriarch did not move; but the stirring of several pairs of wings was heard by me, and two birds from above were instantly seen coming down, intent evidently on fight. The Twit-Twats were certainly preparing to receive them, fully determined to stand their ground and struggle for life even at the risk of death. I thus expected an encounter, when, to my great and pleasant surprise, the patriarch of the hostile tribe came quite out of his recess, not to attack the strangers, but to bid his own progeny stand off. Strange to relate, by a single look at them he drove them away; they evidently felt his power and withdrew to their own uncontested places of refuge. The Twit-Twats, immediately aware that they had found a friend, entered the empty part of the cottage with a look of perfect security. They were saved, and had gained possession, in a manner most unexpected, of comfortable quarters for the winter, where we must leave them for a while.

CHAPTER IV.

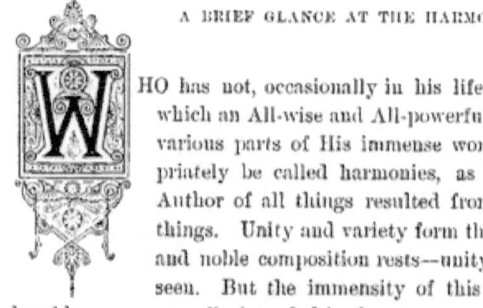

A BRIEF GLANCE AT THE HARMONIES OF CREATION.

WHO has not, occasionally in his life, reflected on the intimate relations which an All-wise and All-powerful Creator has established between the various parts of His immense work? These relations can very appropriately be called harmonies, as if a grand hymn to the Almighty Author of all things resulted from the universal combination of all things. Unity and variety form the two keys on which alone the great and noble composition rests—unity everywhere felt, variety everywhere seen. But the immensity of this subject cannot be embraced in the humble scope naturally intended in these pages. It is far preferable to consider one point only, and leave all others aside. This point is the close analogy existing between human beings and the inferior creatures comprised in the animal kingdom. A most remarkable correlation is directly apparent in their physical organization, and becomes the foundation on which all the systems of natural history are laid. But we discard this branch even of the subject, and confine ourselves to what we think is a superior point of view—namely, to what looks very much like a social, moral, and pedagogical relation between both. This forms, indeed, a harmony of its own kind, *sui generis*, which the history of the Twit-Twats directly presents to the mind of the reader. To be sure, the moral point of view is deficient, since man is the only being on earth susceptible of it; and by this characteristic alone he constitutes an order of his own in nature. The inferior animals are excluded from the moral order. This being well understood, it cannot be denied that animals invariably go so far as to present us the spectacle of a strict observance of law; and the observance of law is a great part of true morality. Hence Holy Scripture refers us often to the remarkable conduct of many inferior beings as an inducement for us to keep God's commandments: "Go to the ant, O sluggard, and consider her ways, and learn wisdom" (Prov. vi. 6); "The bee is small among flying things, but her fruit hath the chiefest sweetness" (Ecclus. xi. 3). If the ant is the pattern of industry, and the bee of lavish generosity, is not the horse the type of courage (Job xxxix. 25)? is not the behemoth that of strength, and the leviathan that of intrepidity?

It would be easy to find in the Old Testament passages where all the human virtues are inculcated by the example of mere animals. But in the New our blessed Lord has gone still further, and has sometimes found in birds and plants inducements for us to practise the highest Christian virtues. "Behold the birds of the air, for they neither sow, nor do they reap, nor gather into barns: and your heavenly Father feedeth them. . . . Consider the lilies of the field how they grow: they labor not, neither do they spin. . . . Be not solicitous, therefore. . . . After all these things do the heathen seek; but your Father knoweth that you have need of all these things" (Matt. vi. passim).

If from morality we pass on to sociability, the harmony established by God Himself between human beings and inferior creatures will appear still much closer and more perfect; for if animals are altogether deprived of true morality, many of them enjoy sociability to a great extent. There is no need here of quoting examples—the simplest books of natural history are full of them; and it is particularly in this line that we shall find in our way instances of a remarkable harmony between sparrows and men.

The same may be said of the pedagogical characteristics which Holy Scripture has particularly in view whenever it touches on the subject. The matter, however, considered in its universality, and as embracing all the branches of the subject, even those which we discard, has been admirably condensed by St. Paul in his Epistle to the Romans, where he says (i. 20): "The invisible things of God, from the creation of the world, are clearly seen, being understood by the things that He made." If even the divine attributes are manifested in visible creation, much more the moral and social peculiarities of man must be typified in inferior beings. Man embodies them in himself, because he is the centre of the material universe, or rather its abridgment, and thus truly deserves the name of *microcosm*, or epitome of creation.

In this little book the intention cannot be to go deeply into this subject, and the reader must expect a gleaning only here and there of some correspondences or congruities existing between a class of birds perfectly familiar to us—the sparrows—and a class of men numerous in this country, and to whom it is good occasionally to draw public attention—namely, European immigrants of all nationalities, but by religion Catholics. The Twit-Twats become thus the shadow of a reality, and all there is to do at the end of this chapter is to prepare the way for their action by briefly showing how human immigration in North America was exactly typified by the various fortunes of the sparrow family.

The "armies of caterpillars," the original occasion of the coming of the birds, may be said to have been, with respect to men, of two distinct and remarkable kinds. First, in the designs of divine Providence, as far as they can be read, the swarms of Catholics arriving from Europe were kindly intended for the gradual reduction and final extinction of the "armies of sects" which, under the pretence of religion, were in fact destroying the moral and eternal happiness of the people. No surer way could be found of planting the Catholic tree on the North American continent than by bringing to it "armies" of sturdy immigrants with the cross in their hands and the true religion of Christ in their hearts.

But as many people outside of the Church would not readily accept the truth of this bright harmony, the ugly "caterpillars" were evidently types of a second though inferior kind, with which harmony no one, even if not a Catholic, can in the least find fault.

The American people, when colonizing this continent, found themselves face to face with two immense obstacles which they alone, with all their astounding energy, could scarcely have surmounted: first, an immense territory as wild as when created, and requiring millions of men to subdue and beautify; and, secondly, an adverse English nation from which war at last had separated them for ever. But even when liberated from the direct control of England they were still left at its mercy by the manufactured goods of every kind they were forced to receive from it. What "army-worm" (such is the name, we think, given in the West to the destructive battalions of caterpillars which often devastate the richest fields) could ever be more terrific and appalling than those two barriers to the progress of a great nation—the uncouth form of the wilderness, the wild vegetation of unprofitable forests and woods eating up the fertility of the soil for no use whatever to mankind; and the voracious rapacity of foreign capitalists and manufacturers, coming with their high-priced products and saying with a sneer: "Take or die"? Where could a remedy be found? The immigrants became for the salvation of a great people what a number of imported little birds turned out to be for the gratification of annoyed and vexed citizens.

The immigrants were first to subdue nature and to render comfortable the dwelling-place of future millions; to connect cities with cities by roads and canals; to render easy the navigation of large rivers hitherto obstructed by sand-bars or snags; to level almost inaccessible mountains, and drain swampy and boggy valleys; to turn into smiling fields gloomy and interminable forests; to raise, all over the surface of an immense territory, private and public structures, at first of an humble but comfortable character, later on of a splendid and varied type, reproducing in the New World the styles of architecture of all times and all countries; to change, in fact, for ever the aspect of a great continent, and replace the few rude traces of roaming and barbarous tribes by the lasting monuments of European civilization.

The second object of that great material mission was not inferior to the first. It was to render the new people settled in this country independent of the monopolizing manufacturers of Europe, chiefly of England, by the erection of factories of every kind, from those of chemical matches to those of mammoth boilers and ironclad monitors. To the inventive genius of the Yankee was to be left the direction of these countless establishments; to the newly-arrived Europeans was entrusted the execution of the plan and the material part of the business. What could the few colonists have done, scattered as they were far and wide over such an immense territory, for the realization of so many vast schemes, had it not been for the armies of starving people every day leaving the shores of Ireland, Germany, England, and other European countries? Let any candid inquirer travel over this new continent and inquire what has been the part everywhere taken by the so-called foreigners in those gigantic enterprises, and he will find that without them the progress to be expected would have been futile and impracticable.

No one, therefore, need be surprised that at first and for a long time these foreigners were as welcome in North America as were subsequently the sparrows when first introduced into the various Atlantic cities. America saw the importance of the muscular help coming to her assistance, and willingly offered to that multitude of new-comers conditions which it would have been perfectly useless for them to expect in their own country. Hence they flocked hither in immense numbers.

What rendered this mutual good feeling more natural was the fact that the population of the United States was composed, from the first, of men of all countries and races. They could not think, therefore, of excluding any nationality whatever, especially when there were so many weighty reasons for admitting all with open arms.

It was only later on that an opposition at first began to manifest itself, silently, it is true, but which gradually swelled to proportions of unexpected magnitude, first in the Native-American party of 1843, and afterward in the Know-nothing organization of 1856. And, strange to say, the motives of that opposition partook a great deal of the nature of the war declared against the inoffensive birds so warmly admitted at first to the privacy of American families. The birds were noisy, so were the immigrants; the birds were vulgar, so the new-comers undoubtedly were; the birds multiplied too fast, so the foreigners threatened to do; the birds showed themselves too much at home, and interfered too much with the staid, quiet habits of Yankeedom, so the foreigners were accused of doing; the birds, though strangers to the country, were already driving away the native robins and *chippies*, who could not build their nests in the neighborhood of the sparrows. All such annoyances and irritating grievances were likewise attributed to the presence of the so-called foreigners—namely, the immigrants from Europe—so that no one can refuse to admit that the Twit-Twats were a type and the foreigners a sad reality.

But the chief cause of the violent hatred of Nativists and Know-nothings for everybody not born on these shores was their religion, for a great part of these foreigners were Catholics. What a terrible verdict against the mother Church was then rendered by many *patriotic* Americans! Ignorance, despotism, hatred of civilization, etc., were reproached to the Bride of Christ, and in the eyes of those who thus spoke and wrote it amounted to a perfect demonstration. So likewise it has been seen that the main reason which turned the tide of popular feeling against the poor sparrows was the unexpected discovery that most of them came from the ruins of Catholic monasteries. The Twit-Twats in particular had been brought from the steeple of a Catholic church in Ireland, and not, as people at first fondly imagined, from the factories of Birmingham or Manchester, or from the prim rectories of Essex and Sussex, in Protestant England.

This general statement of well-known facts was necessary for the thorough understanding of what is to follow.

Harmonies of Creation between Men and Birds.

CHAPTER V.

A DESCRIPTION OF SOME STRANGE NATURAL HABITS OF THE TWIT-TWATS CONSIDERED AS TYPES OF HUMAN BEINGS.

NOW that the old native pair, together with the ancient Twit-Twat couple, are lodged in the little wooden house in one of the Lombardy poplars near my windows, each of them occupying its cell in close contiguity, I can study their habits to the best advantage. It is easy for me to see them going in or coming out, hopping on the little platform in front of their cottage, interchanging courtesies or the reverse, flying about on the trees around, or down on the ground and in the street, and showing their feelings—shall I say their thoughts?—by what they do or avoid doing. The numerous progeny of the native patriarchs is strongly established on the top of the rectory or in other poplar-trees which I myself had long before planted in front of the house. The Twit-Twats' numerous offspring live still in the *façade* of St. Joseph's Convent, and their usual haunts cannot be seen from my windows, as they are situated precisely east of Fourth Street, back of the rectory; but they often come to visit me, and, as was previously seen, their demeanor is quite different from that of the native birds. This little picture must remain in the mind of the reader for the understanding of what is immediately to follow.

From the elevated position I occupied in this small world I could observe everything to perfection, and had no need of consulting other people, reading books of natural history, or having recourse to dusty and ancient tomes describing sparrows and robins.

I had, however, one excess to avoid—I mean being carried away by my imagination so far as to make of my little friends so many real men and women. This is what Lafontaine has done in his *Fables*. Read even the first, "La Cigale et la Fourmi"; how they talk! how they address and answer each other! You at once imagine two human inhabitants of this mundane sphere, one of them an improvident spendthrift, the other a prudent husbandman attentive to his larder and provisions. Still, everybody reads Lafontaine and finds him charming. I certainly can never hope to have as many readers; though if I were fond enough of vainglory I might try my best to imitate him in every respect. But I have a conscience and cannot condescend to lie too outrageously. I must even say frankly to those who will do me the favor of reading this little book that, if whatever I describe as having been seen by me is true to the letter, if the strange doings of either the strangers or the natives have happened exactly as I describe them, the same cannot be said altogether of the inner motives which I sometimes assign to those exterior actions. I may have been mistaken in this, for it is difficult to read the thoughts of sparrows, even supposing sparrows to have thoughts. Thus everybody is warned beforehand, and we can resume the thread of our story.

The old Twit-Twats were *probably* so much fatigued when they took possession of their new quarters that during the whole afternoon and evening of that Christmas day they did not come out of their cell; they spent the time inside on a wretched straw bed, *certainly*, since they had not had time to bring on new hay, and the cell had not been occupied for several years before. But at least they remained quiet, though with an empty craw and stomach. The obstreperous native progeny did not dare to attack them so soon, and the venerable native patriarchs did not think it was becoming to disturb them in the sad interior of their dwelling.

Thus this first Christmas holiday was cheerless enough for the poor birds, and they had no idea whatever of the happy, nay, brilliant, one which Providence had in store for them a twelvemonth hence.

When, after an early breakfast on the morning of St. Stephen's day, I looked out of my window, old Mr. Twit-Twat was just coming out of his hole for the first time, and he was alone! Mrs. Twit-Twat, to my great regret, did not appear. Was she dead? It is a great pity that man has not yet found a means of entering into communication with animals, not by articulate speech, since they are incapable of it, but at least by sure signs on which people could rely. The pretended interchange of compliments between the master and his dog, the rider and his horse, etc., is only a sham, as many grave philosophers have proved, though Lafontaine is emphatically of another opinion.

So that I could not learn from old Mr. Twit-Twat what had happened to his consort in her place of refuge; and it would have been cruel to plant a ladder against the tree for the purpose of ascertaining the truth. I preferred to wait patiently for further developments.

Soon Mr. Twit-Twat became very active. As he must have been really hungry, his first concern was to fill his stomach; and, in spite of the snow on the ground, he did it without difficulty, for I had already the evening before charitably spread a great quantity of crumbs at the foot of his tree. But after he had fully attended to himself I was greatly surprised to see him go back to his cell, remain a few moments inside, come out again, and repeat the same operation again and again during a part of the forenoon. I was, therefore, sure of one thing—that Mrs. Twit-Twat was not dead; for, on the contrary supposition, the old gentleman would not have acted as he did. It is known that

Domestic Habits of the Twit-Twats.

a hole in a wall occupied by the dead body of a bird will never be visited by another. Do birds respect the sacredness of the tomb? We cannot judge of their feelings, but it is hard to explain it otherwise, unless it comes from their cowardice at the image of grim death.

In his trips up and down he acted exactly as birds do in summer when the female is hatching. Was he bringing her food? I could not exactly answer this question, for I am somewhat near-sighted and was unable to see whether he brought anything or not.

And during that forenoon what were the native colony doing all around? Several of the birds settled on the top of the church attempted again to pounce upon our friend; but he showed fight, and, being now well fed, proved himself a still vigorous fellow in spite of his previous privations. The feeling of animosity on the part of the native party was not extinct—far from it. But old Mr. Twit-Twat had a beak and claws, and could defend himself. Besides this, the old patriarch near him continued friendly; and although he did not so actively protect him as he had done the day before—knowing, I suppose, that our friend was plucky enough to take care of himself—still it was a check to his numerous progeny to show, as he did, that he willingly allowed free quarters to his neighbor. These were the various circumstances which I witnessed on the morning of St. Stephen's day; and I confess that I became very much interested in that study. As if the tones of a sweet harmony had delighted my ears, I was almost riveted to the place, and would, perhaps, have forgotten my dinner had not the voice of duty called me away.

In the afternoon, as soon as free, I was again at my post; and, indeed, the spectacle that offered itself to me, more puzzling still than that of the forenoon, became more attractive also—in fact, almost fascinating. It was furnished this time by the old female native bird, who had taken no part in the Twit-Twats' defence the day before.

She was always sedate and gentle, but on that afternoon of St. Stephen's day appeared more so than usual, and I remarked with a great deal of astonishment that, after fluttering around a little, she finally entered the room of our friends, and went, no doubt, to visit the poor female stranger. Old Twit-Twat was near at the time, and appeared at first unwilling to allow her such a liberty, which everybody knows is not at all in their usual manners. He was on the point of driving her off even, when he saw her venerable mate perched on the top of the cottage, evidently surprised that his former services to the Twit-Twats should be repaid by ingratitude, and ready to call back our friend to his senses by, I suppose, a good knock-down. On reflection, therefore, old Twit-Twat became wiser and more sociable, and allowed Mrs. Native to have her free *entrées* to his *sanctum*. She used the permission, to my knowledge, quite frequently. What she did within cannot be said, nor even imagined; but, after all I have seen of the doings of animals, I should not be in the least surprised if she was actually comforting and feeding the sick bird. Long ago I have imagined that the well-known lines of Shakspere could be very well applied to many strange antics of birds, and even snakes:

> There are more things in heaven and earth, Horatio,
> Than are dreamt of in your philosophy."

Instinct in animals is essentially different from moral feeling in man; and I beg the reader to believe that I do not share in the infatuation of the modern evolutionists, who confound one with the other. But it can be said without fear of heterodoxy that instinct in animals often supplies the place of what is moral feeling in man. Who has ever looked at two doves petting one another, and has not immediately conceived that their attachment, produced by nothing higher than instinct, is the exact reproduction of the far holier feeling of love in man? Who has seen a mother-bird feeding her young without imagining that he has under his eyes an example offered by God Himself to the mother of a human family who owes herself entirely to her children? Nay, more, in the words of Moses (Deut. xxxii. 11), the Almighty compares His love for Israel to that of "the eagle enticing her young to fly, and hovering over them, spreading her wings, taking them up, and carrying them on her shoulders."

And it is not family instinct only which is remarkable in animals. We have often read of the deep attachment of a dog for his master, of an elephant for his keeper, of a lioness for her saviour, etc.—an attachment carried occasionally as far as death itself. Can we not suppose that a sparrow may feel deeply the misfortunes of a fellow-bird? What motive could have led Mrs. Native to enter into the room of Mrs. Twit-Twat, except it were to afford consolation? This set me thinking the whole afternoon and a good part of the following night.

Meanwhile, although saved from destruction, the Twit-Twats were far from comfortable in their new quarters, and this time they shared their troubles with other sparrows. There were a great number of them hopping and flying and twittering about the roof of the church and the front of the convent and the rectory. The sisters saw very few of them in their garden, and these occasionally received some crumbs—enough for them. But the others had mainly to depend upon what remained of the *screenings*—the word may not be correct, but it is so expressive here—thrown twice a day to fifteen or twenty fowls belonging to the parsonage. Everything else which could fill the stomach of sparrows was buried under a foot and a half of snow; and I have never observed them to feed on the buds of trees, as other birds are said to do. Hence I am sure that they had often to go to sleep at night with a more than half empty stomach. They say that fasting is not very painful in warm countries; but wherever the cold is intense all acknowledge that starving is a very unpleasant sensation. At this time the sensation must have been familiar to the birds.

There was, moreover, a great hardship to which I have often seen the poor Twit-Twats exposed. The morning after their first night in the cottage the old bird found the way of egress somewhat barred by snow; but as it was very soft, he passed through it as "through a mist." The same was repeated on several occasions. But much oftener the furious wind had so compressed and hardened the snow that the bird had to use his beak and claws for hours together to open a hole large enough to get through into his cottage. I was frequently a witness to this when a storm during the day had blocked up the entrance. Poor Twit-Twat, coming back late in the afternoon to retire for the night, had to knock and knock with his little beak, and scratch and scratch with his little claws, to open a passage. He never failed to apply his mechanical powers in the right place, and when he had dug through the hard snow for two or three inches he was sure at last to find the blessed passage open. He was more cunning in that respect than many blundering carpenters, who, after spending a good deal of time cutting a hole in the outside of a frame building, find at last that their operation has been carried on a foot or so to the right or left of the required place, and have to begin again. The Twit-Twats never had such a disheartening mishap; their previous calculations were always right, and the little passage they dug in the snow, although never larger than the hole in the cottage, always corresponded exactly with it, as if they had used rule, and compass, and all that sort of thing.* But in spite of this inerrancy of calculation, what an amount of trouble it gave the poor birds to be there, half fed, exposed to the cold wind after a day of frequent disappointments, hammering and hammering for at least an hour and a half—I have measured the time, watch in hand, on two occasions at least—and after all this labor to find inside a half-handful of straw, and even this powdered with the snow that had been blown through the too visible chinks in the cottage!

Days went on, however, and finally on a beautiful January morning two birds came out together, and at last the long-lost female Twit-Twat appeared, as active and frisky as ever. The labor would henceforth be done doubly as quick, and happiness would in due time come back again to the desolate couple.

Before this chapter is closed a word of explanation is required to meet a probable objection. The reader might say, "Your analogy, Mr. Author, is already wrong. You wish to prove the opposition of the Native party to Catholic immigrants, and some of your native birds are, at the very start, the best friends of the strangers. Why is this thus? as Artemus Ward used to say."

My answer will prove, I hope, satisfactory. It has been said that all Americans were at first strangers from Europe. None of them are really natives of the soil by race. Those, however, whose ancestors have for a long time resided in this country—it goes sometimes to a couple of centuries—may very well be called natives, as is done in this story. Everybody knows that there are two kinds of such citizens. Some—many, in my opinion—were not opposed to the arrival of new immigrants; nay, I have personally known a number of them who were constantly their best friends and helpers. But there were others who were not so liberal-minded. They were known in this coun-

---

* The reader will please believe that all the details I give of the doings of the birds anywhere in these pages have actually fallen under my observation, and that I invent nothing. It is only when I assign motives to the birds, and suppose them acting intelligently, that I use the privilege of a philosophical historian; then the reader may believe or not, as he chooses.

try as the Native party, or rather faction. The two sorts cannot be put in the same category. Our story, therefore, is perfectly consistent.

It has been even remarked that many members of the Native American or Know-nothing party were themselves only lately arrived on this continent; and these, pretending to be natives, showed themselves the most fanatical opponents of more honest strangers and aliens.

CHAPTER VI.

THE BEGINNING OF A FIERCE BATTLE BETWEEN TWO HOSTILE TRIBES OF BIRDS.

JANUARY was near its end; according to the almanac, the days were growing longer in the afternoon, though very little longer, if at all, in the morning—an anomaly in nature. The old Twit-Twat couple, since first coming out together, were fast recovering from their previous weakness, and appeared to enjoy the good fare daily offered them in the barn-yard. The native patriarchs, it must be said, showed little change, and their sedateness was, if anything, suddenly increased by the surprising absence of most of their progeny. There were now few, indeed, of these turbulent birds to annoy the old pair, or to oblige their patriarch to prove his authority over them. The same was nearly the case with the young Twit-Twats, most of whom had disappeared from the church-roof, and particularly from the row of Lombardy poplars, which now loomed up in their solitary grandeur.

What could be the cause of it? This question was puzzling to my reasoning faculties, and I did not know how to find the answer to it. Were we to be deprived of our agreeable company for any length of time, and perhaps for ever? The answer came to me the next time I went to the convent. It was a part of my office to visit the nuns once a week, and the first day I entered I could not account for the number of birds I saw in their garden and all around about. The reader remembers, perhaps, that few had ventured thither previously. Many of the turbulent natives, it is true, had settled since Christmas day in the front of the convent, after driving away some Twit-Twats who had previously lived there—a circumstance I had forgotten to mention. This new move was probably in retaliation for the admittance of the Twit-Twat patriarchs into the midst of their former colony—nay, into the very cottage of their chief. But if they were thus numerous in the front of the house, it was only recently that it had become so. Hitherto a few natives used to fly over the convent building and alight in the interior of the garden, so that the good sisters could easily feed the forlorn birds whenever they ventured into their grounds. But now they were coming in great troops, and very noisy they were. When I asked the reverend mother the cause, she did not know. Quite lately, she said, swarms of them had come from the other side of Fourth

Street, and by their screams they disturbed the whole community. The nuns had welcomed the few stragglers that first arrived. Now they took good care not to feed this multitude. All they wished was that the troublesome visitors should go away and leave them in peace and quiet, as they had been before. That was the substance of the reverend mother's explanation.

It was puzzling indeed, and in order to study the problem, which interested me a great deal, I made up my mind to remain in the convent after finishing my business with the nuns. The Sisters of St. Joseph are not cloistered, and there was no rule to prevent me from entering their house, their garden and all its nooks and corners, and the most hidden recesses of a shanty or two which had remained there ever since they purchased the property.

I was not long in finding out the cause of the difficulty between the birds. It came from the deep-seated animosity which I already knew. It was the beginning of a bloody feud which might have the most serious consequences for the miserable birds; or rather it was the first strategic movement of a campaign which might last the whole winter. I had heard and read of pitched battles among the sparrows, and was, perhaps, to witness something of the kind on the largest scale.

The reader is aware that from the first, had it not been for the noble exception of the patriarchs, natives and Twit-Twats would have been declared by any ethnologist to be two irreconcilable races, and every one knows what this means. But for what particular reason had the young Twit-Twats lately attacked the native birds and driven them from the convent façade into the garden, as they had done only a few days before? Was it because the natives frequently came to feed from the *screenings* scattered in the barnyard of the rectory, which, being east of the church, the Twit-Twats might have considered as belonging to their territory; or was it the effect of a long-nourished spirit of retaliation for the inexcusable conduct of the whole native brood toward the old Twit-Twat couple which had nearly ended in their death on Christmas day? I could not say what was the cause of the war, but that there was now a state of war there could not be the least doubt.

If the reader wishes to investigate the subject scientifically he will find that, according to the best naturalists of the day who have studied their habits, there are occasionally fearful battles among sparrows. He will meet in those books the formal statement that the birds assemble, often to the number of many hundreds, on the roof of some large edifice and then engage in furious combat. The two parties, they say, are easily distinguished from each other. The birds appear to adhere to the one side from the first; they never desert their flag, nor do they change sides even at the end of the struggle. There must evidently be a great cause of conflict, common to many individuals, which all have espoused with ardor, and which they pursue to the end either of victory or defeat. What naturalists say of this resembles so much what takes place among men that, in my opinion, if the sparrows had, in their process of evolution, invented the art of writing they might have chronicles of their exploits pretty much like

Beginning of a Battle over the Convent.

ours. Something like the Trojan war, or the deadly struggle between the Persians and Greeks in the time of Xerxes, might amuse the spare hours of sparrows when they have done hatching their broods in summer and go rusticating, *as they certainly do.*

Long ago, in my native country, I had heard from common report of the fearful battles between sparrows which country-people sometimes observe in the suburbs of large towns in France. Either on the roof of a capacious barn, or, better still, in the vicinity of a windmill, according to rumor, they congregate in thousands; but I suppose Dame Rumor exaggerates as usual, and that we must read hundreds when she writes thousands. For in the old country such feats of daring among Liliputian bipeds are not recorded in scientific books, nor are they loudly trumpeted in any veracious newspaper even. In this country, however, public opinion is more carefully instructed and formed by the journalists and naturalists, so that, besides treatises on natural history, the daily journals accurately register all that occurs in the cities or towns; and I remember well in particular that a severe conflict between sparrows was reported in full in the spring of 1863, a few years before the occurrence of which I now speak, in a Troy paper—the Troy *Whig*, I think—which I daily received for my personal instruction. It seems that several dozens of sparrows were killed in that early fight. Bird-battles I had, therefore, read about and pondered over, but never had I personally witnessed anything of the kind. Now I was to enjoy such a privilege, and I did my best to become acquainted with all the particulars.

I had come just in the nick of time. From the reverend mother's narrative, there had been so far only what may be called skirmishing; but when I took a favorable position for an exact observation of the whole field, I immediately remarked that the Twit-Twats, having driven away the natives from the front of the house, were drawn up on the top of the sisters' convent, their backs turned west toward Fourth Street, and they were all looking east in the direction of a frame building which stood beyond the sisters' garden, along Trenton Street. On the top of the frame building the native brood were already in battle array. The Twit-Twats appeared to be the aggressors; and, having penetrated so far into the enemy's territory, they seemed determined to drive him altogether from the sisters' premises along toward the east into the wild grounds of the County Poorhouse, which is not far off. Had this plan succeeded the victorious Twit-Twats would have been able to enjoy in peace not only the sacred ground around the church and the rectory, occupied by them since Christmas, but also the holy and pleasant retreat where the nuns, during the hours of recreation, were accustomed to rest from their labors. It was evidently a grand object and worth fighting for.

But it was just this which inspired the native battalions with the courage of despair; and when their enemies approached them on the top of the frame house which was their last resting-place on their former grounds, it became at once a hand-to-hand, or rather a claw-to-claw, conflict, the result of which appeared doubtful from the beginning. The better to understand the details of this fierce engagement, it is proper to know that this frame house was used by the sisters—and is used yet, I think—as an infant school. Behind it, along Trenton Street, a stage had been erected for the amusement of the children, and served them for their infantine gymnastic exercises. There were many wooden steps up which the babies could march singing in unison, and at the top of the steps was a large platform on which they could exercise to advantage when the weather was fine and the sun shone.

After a quarter of an hour's severe fighting and shrill screaming in that place the Twit-Twats found, to their cost, that a good general is necessary when an army thinks of invading an enemy's territory, and they had no general. Old Twit-Twat was still in his cottage. I myself saw with dismay—for I do not conceal the side to which I leaned—that the Twit-Twats would have immediately to retreat, if they wished to continue longer as a race. A good many pairs of them had already fallen from the roof of the frame house, and were rolling down the steps of the gymnasium, pursued by the infuriated natives.

There was nothing for them to do but to retreat in good order while there was yet time to do so. They fell back, as military writers say, to the Fourth Street side of the top of the convent, which but half an hour before they had left with the highest hopes of victory. Here it is good to let them rest for a moment.

During this short recess it is proper to remark that when an army has been driven back from an advanced position, and has been obliged to reoccupy its previous one, a wager can be laid of five to one that this army is in great danger of being defeated a second time on account of *demoralization*, to use another military term. This could be proved by a hundred examples taken from the campaigns of Charlemagne a thousand years ago, from those of Napoleon I. at the beginning of this century, without speaking of the civil war in our own country not many years ago. Thus the Twit-Twats had a poor chance, and they did well to rest, though it were for a few moments only, while the natives prepared to attack them again and drive them entirely out of their territory.

This was but the affair of a few instants, for the poor Twit-Twats were still fluttering with dismay and had not fully recovered their natural courage. Again several pairs of them rolled down from the roof of the convent and fell into Fourth Street on the other side. In the meantime the main body retreated across the street in such terror that they did not even attempt to take a new position on the church, which was a little farther west and certainly formed a part of their dominion. They flew over and beyond it, coming down on the other side and alighting in the Lombardy poplars, where they thought themselves secure against the possibility of an attack. They imagined, poor little fools, that their enemies would be satisfied with the immense advantages already gained and would content themselves with taking possession again of their whole former ground. In fact, the natives' movements appeared to give color to that opinion, for they began to twitter in great glee, as if they were singing a final song of triumph, as is usual after a victory. But I had a more correct notion of their greedy spirit; I knew they would think of at once wresting from the Twit-Twats their new hard-gained position, and would invade the broad acres that lay west of Third Street as far as Second, and further. I therefore concluded to go home, where I could better observe the future movements of the two armies, which were now to take place under my windows. But it is good to mention incidentally that before I left the convent grounds many of the sisters came to me with their hands full of sparrows. In the goodness of their hearts they had visited the scene of the first conflict around the children's gymnasium, and found many poor Twit-Twats there who were already reviving from their wounds and fainting fits, so that there was every prospect of a full recovery for them. The fact is that, after the most rigorous search, only *one* corpse could be discovered, which, after all, was probably not a very great loss for the Twit-Twat army.

On this first breaking out of hostilities the thoughtless Twit-Twats were guilty of the same imprudence which was generally observed in this country on the occasion of the various conflicts between Catholic immigrants and the Native American non-Catholic faction. They *appeared* to be the aggressors. This has just been said of the birds, and it was repeated *ad nauseam* by the Know-nothing papers of the United States whenever Catholic immigrants were pounced upon, beaten, killed, their houses burned as at Louisville, their churches destroyed as at Philadelphia, or their religious institutions burned down as at Boston, etc., etc. Aggressors! How could they be? All they asked was to be allowed "to enjoy life, liberty, and the pursuit of happiness," which, according to the Declaration of Independence, are justly called the inalienable rights of man. To an impartial observer it is clear that the conflict was forced both upon the foreign birds and the foreign men. But we must hasten on and describe the sequel of a conflict which has so far only begun. This will be the object of the next chapter.

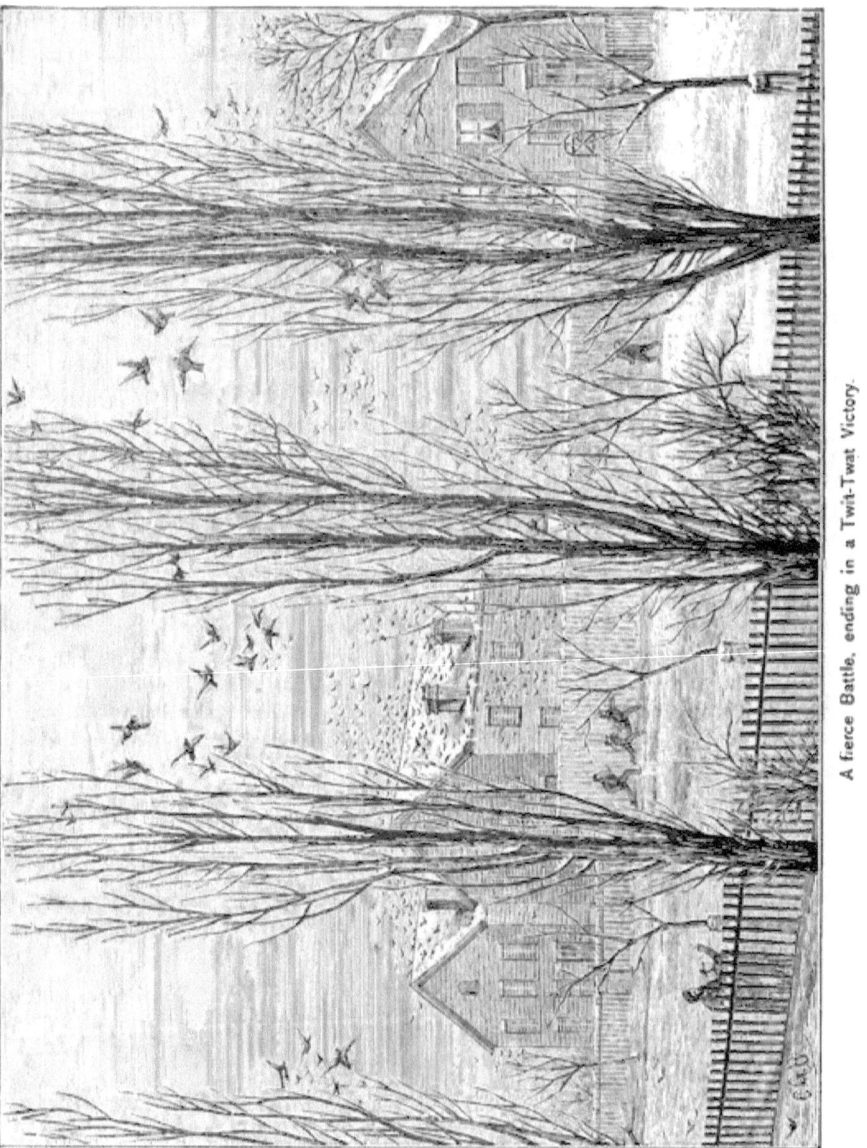

A fierce Battle, ending in a Twit-Twat Victory.

CHAPTER VII.

A GLORIOUS BATTLE-FIELD AND THE FIRST GREAT TWIT-TWAT VICTORY.

HAD been scarcely a quarter of an hour in my room when I perceived that my anticipations of what the native troops would try to do were about to be realized. They had felt bold enough, as was seen, to press forward with vigor in the first flush of their victory—ay, to leave their own ground and invade that of the Twit-Twats. For some time I could hardly understand what really was going on, for the main conflict was then raging over my head on the roof of the parsonage, and but few birds were as yet fighting in the poplars. Soon, however, the state of things was apparent, for down from the roof to the trees came both natives and Twit-Twats with a rush. Thenceforth I could distinctly see them, as they were a few feet only from my windows. The poplars fairly bent beneath their weight, and there was not a branch, not a twig of the trees upon which there were not several of them, and all furiously fighting, and mostly in pairs. Did I but know the names of the individuals I might describe many a passage at arms between heroes of the contending armies, as Homer has done in his celebrated *Iliad*. One, at least, of them I did recognize, and this was the venerable Twit-Twat patriarch whom I had so often before studied with attention. He was there, though he had not been of the expedition to the convent. But no doubt he was aware that his numerous progeny were now fighting *pro aris et focis*, and that at this perilous moment it was his duty as chieftain to be at their head. The gentle native patriarch did not join his side in the fray from reasons that, considering his past conduct, we can well imagine—chiefly, perhaps, from the repugnance he always felt to the turbulence and bad manners of his own young colony.

Old Mr. Twit-Twat began at once to put order into his battalions. As he flew constantly from one side of the battle-field to the other, it was easy to conjecture that his only object was *organization*; and, in fact, I immediately remarked a great change in the ranks of the Twit-Twats. They no longer gave way before the enemy, but held their ground with a great deal of steadfastness and intrepidity. The ardor of their chief was evidently animating them, and they seemed to have altogether forgotten their previous defeat.

Then a remarkable sight met my eyes. Each poplar-tree formed a distinct field of contention. In our human way of speaking of military affairs we should say that each tree contained an organized battalion, and if you embraced in the compass of your vision several trees together it looked exactly like what, in military parlance, is called a *division*. Had you made a further step in point of combination you would have before you an army corps. I beg my reader to believe that there is nothing far-fetched in these expressions. They represent exactly what fell under my personal observation during that remarkable day. On the native side, it must be remarked, there did not appear to be anything like the order, the strategic combination, the weighty concentration which the Twit-Twats offered to human eyes. And, indeed, there was nothing surprising in this: they had no chief.

The result was as sure as fate. Victory perched on the Twit-Twat standard; but the process took some time for its full accomplishment, and we have still to describe the various steps through which it passed.

And first there was a general retreat on the part of the natives. This time the Twit-Twats did not push their enemies back eastward to their own former grounds around the sisters' convent. Whatever may have been the motive, they drove them gradually in the very contrary direction—that is, towards the west. It looked as if they maliciously intended to push them on towards the Hudson River, which is not very far off, and there mercilessly drown them. The native birds, however, did not go so far in their flight. They found just on the further side of Third Street, at the edge of a waste field extending to the very sidewalk of Second Street, a rather large brick house in full view from my windows, and their disordered bands rested on this house. This was the second stage of the movement.

Their distance from me at that point was greater than on any previous occasion; still, I could perfectly distinguish everything without the help of an opera-glass, though I had borrowed one from a friend at the very beginning of these accurate observations. The Twit-Twats followed their enemies, who kept huddled together. It was push, drive, and hurl forward, until the Twit-Twats at length took possession of a large frame building contiguous to the one of brick occupied by the native troops.

I remarked with pleasure that not only old Mr. Twit-Twat was there commanding his troops, but even Mrs. Twit-Twat herself, now fully recovered, had placed herself at the head of a great number of female warriors, whom it was easy to distinguish from the males by the subdued colors of their heads and wings. It was evident that, as this was to be a decisive action, the whole nation was roused, and the gentler sex even was going to display its valor. I imagined that I saw before me a noble troop of Amazons, and the wonderful story related by ancient authors, which used to make us laugh when we were at school, did not appear on this occasion to be so perfectly ludicrous.

The two armies, raised on high between the earth and the skies, and perched on their respective houses, stood a moment in silence fronting each other. Then the fray began. On the native side there was no order whatever, for they had no one to lead them; but there was in their breasts a deep feeling of obstinacy which might be called the courage of despair. After having been so long victorious, to see themselves in this hopeless condition, their former ground almost out of sight, and the river near them in the west ominously rolling its dark waters as a cold bath in which they might be submerged! There was enough in all their present surroundings to freeze the blood in their veins, or rather to send it violently rushing to their heads and impel them to the most violent resolves. Soon you could see the battalions on both sides advancing, and retreating, and fighting. But what struck me most at the beginning of this furious battle was the incredible amount of screaming. It was worse than the shrill squeaks that you hear in the early July mornings, when the sparrows begin the day by a loud concert sufficient to awaken the most heavy slumberers; it was worse even than the harsh screams which you sometimes hear issue from the throats of two male birds fighting almost to extinction at the top of a tall tree over your head; it was the harshest confusion of shrill sounds, as if their throats had been made of brass and their beaks of adamant. Nothing but a foreign language can express it, and the French have the best simile that can be found, although it does not yet come up to the reality: *C'était un énorme timbre de voix*, filling the air with discord and striking the ear of the listener with a piercing pang.

In spite of the *supersparrow** courage of the natives it was evident that their want of discipline consequent upon the total absence of a commander would be in the end fatal to their cause. Owing to the ability of old General Twit-Twat on the other side not even a corporal's squad of the natives could at any time obtain a footing on the frame house on which the Irish birds had established their headquarters; and soon enough, on the contrary, a whole Irish battalion pushed their advancing columns up to the very top of the brick edifice where the natives had proudly planted their flag. That advanced part of the hostile Twit-Twat army comprised even a full regiment of Amazons, though old Mrs. Twit-Twat could not be seen there and remained among her friends. I presume her old mate had refused her the permission to risk her precious life in so hazardous a position.

But at any rate the Irish warriors forced their way into the very midst of their enemies, who soon appeared doomed to instant defeat. A circumstance, however, very fortunate for them delayed that fatal moment a little while longer. It has been said that the two edifices were contiguous to each other. This, however, must be somewhat qualified. Owing to the projection of the cornices a space of about two feet had been left between the two buildings; and it happened that the chimneys of both raised their flues in close contiguity to each other. This afforded a great advantage to the despairing natives, and they might even hope that this peculiarity of construction would be the means of allowing them to invade a part of the Twit-Twat quarters. A fierce struggle, therefore, was soon going on around the chimney-flues. It was there, it

---

* We are not fond of neology; still, when it is a matter of necessity a new word must be coined. We say, speaking of our own race, *superhuman courage*; why not *supersparrow courage* when we have to speak of these little birds?

is true, that the chief carnage of the native birds took place, but many a Twit-Twat also bit the ground in the same dangerous spot. When a bird on either side was exhausted, and could no longer keep his balance on the edge of the roof, he fell down between the two houses, and there was scarcely any hope of his soon reviving and reappearing on the same battle-field. After a short time I noticed that there was a perfect hecatomb of victims, and it was principally in this way that the ranks on both sides were thinned. But the losses were invariably much greater in the native army. It was evident that by this process the contest would soon be ended, and that through the want of warriors on the defeated side there would, within about half an hour from the onset, be but little fighting. This saved the native troops, however, for they could not be driven to the river and drowned *en masse;* and it was clear, besides, that many of those who had fallen in the conflict would in course of time revive and resume the thread of their exploits. Thus our story is not yet finished, for many other important events will have to be recorded before the final triumph of the good cause.

The reader may ask why I did not go to the very spot of the "hecatomb" directly after the struggle was over, and then and there see to the revival of my friends the Twit-Twats, and to the complete extinction of life in their enemies. A good moral reason for abstaining from it could be given, which, however, was not the true one. I might say that if during life it is easy to distinguish the members of each party, it is not the same when they are either dead or in a fainting condition; so that I should have scarcely been able to decide which to revive and which to strangle. But there was another and better reason. It was at the end of January, if I mistake not. A deep, hard-frozen snow, which had, in fact, been turned to ice, lay spread all over the street, but particularly along and between the two houses. I should have had to put on a pair of skates; this, it is true, I might have done, but I could not skate, having never in my life learned how to enjoy that healthful exercise. Let the reader accept this excuse, and allow me to proceed with the narrative of that important engagement.

The native troops were for this time completely routed, and the Twit-Twats, while singing their pæan of triumph, knew they would for a long time be left in peace to feed on the fat of the land, and to multiply indefinitely to the great advantage of their race. There is scarcely any need of remarking that this has also been invariably the case with the European immigrants. Whatever may have been the trials they had on many occasions to undergo, they have always overcome them in the end, acquired power and influence in the country they had adopted, and have become at last true American citizens. If a number of them have been unequal to the task and have perished ingloriously, the mass has succeeded beyond any human expectation, and to this day many of them are an honor to their original country and religion.

In concluding this chapter I anticipate a strong objection on the part of the reader. It may be said: "In opening your book, Mr. Author, we thought that the renowned Twit-Twats, for whom you have such deep predilection, were to give us the example of all the Christian virtues, and we still remember the texts you quoted from

Holy Scripture to prove that Almighty God has given the animals their instinct in order to teach men true wisdom, etc., etc. Now, is not the conduct of your pets scandalous? And if your readers feel any pleasure in this little book, will they not be tempted to imitate your brave heroes and to adopt the same life of depredation and bloodshed, etc., etc.?" This objection I have constantly had before my eyes, and I must answer it in my own plain way; prefixing, however, the reflection, made once before, that this is a serious matter, and that we are not now in the domain of the ludicrous. This is not to be met with a laugh.

The Twit-Twats, and in general all animals, are, as it were, perfect in their instinct. They always strictly obey the laws of their nature, and thus, although themselves deprived of a moral law, they can teach us morality. If they ever commit any excess in eating, drinking, etc., it is always at the instigation of man, when, being reduced to a state of servitude which is often called domesticity, they are placed in conditions altogether abnormal to their nature, and are forced to indulge in appetites which they never show in a state of freedom. Thus the poor goose is fed in such a manner that her liver becomes larger and heavier than the remainder of her body, in order to tickle the palate of a miserable epicure. Go through all the trumpeted cases of excess in animals, and you will find that man is at the bottom of it. Man alone, in fact, has been touched by original sin and disobeys the commands of his God.

It is only the state of almost universal war existing among creatures inferior to man which could create a serious difficulty; and it is well known that John Stuart Mill thought he had found in it a strong basis for his deplorable and disgraceful atheism. Protestant theologians have supposed that the whole of creation was affected by the sin of Adam. I do not think that the Church has ever consecrated this opinion, which you will not find in any Catholic dogmatical treatises. War among men is undoubtedly, as well as death, the effect of our first parents' disobedience. None would have died if sin had not first stepped in. But even in case man had not prevaricated war would have existed among animals, since the carnivorous species have received their teeth and their stomachs at their first creation, and they feed on flesh. Animals have not been given for food to man only, but they must devour each other, since for many of them there is no other way to live than to prey upon others.

It has been proved by naturalists of repute that in the greater number of cases it is for a large number of them the least painful way of ending their life. Sudden death, which for man must be dreadful, on account of his expectation of a hereafter, is for animals only the sudden deliverance from infirmity and sickness, against which there is no other provision; and the speedy ending of their troubles under the tiger's claws or within the eagle's sharp talons is often a real blessing for the poor kid or the miserable shepherd's dog. Mr. Mill supposes that if God exists everything must be absolutely faultless, as if created things partook of the divine nature and were not naturally and necessarily subject to imperfection. Give us your plan, Mr. Mill, and please tell us what you would have done if it had been your business to create the world. You would probably have been as successful as Laplace, who found fault with the text of Genesis which says that the moon was made to give light to man during the darkness of night; and he pretended that such a position in the heavens, and such a way of arranging the various orbits of sun, moon, and earth, could be found as that our satellite would much better fulfil its function than it does at present. A simple Jesuit—Father Caraffa—proved mathematically that in Laplace's beautiful arrangement the moon would scarcely have given us the light which a rush candle furnishes to the peasant in his cabin. On the contrary, whoever knows what obstacles matter and sin offer to the benign designs of the Creator cannot but marvel how He has surmounted the difficulty and brought about the greatest amount of good in spite of the stubborn opposition of evil. The wise Englishman—Mr. Mill—it is true, was of opinion that he himself could have dispensed with evil altogether. But he showed by this that he little knew what evil really is, although all the time complaining of it. Had he read what St. Augustine has said of its nature he would have understood that to dispense with evil would have required God to desist from creating anything and from giving existence to any being outside of Himself. *Evil*, according to all true metaphysicians, is nothing in itself, and cannot be comprehended except as the limitation of *good*, which alone has a real existence. Hence all contingent—that is, created—beings, because they are limited, must partake of evil in some sense or other. And, mind, there is no need for this of supposing dualism. On the contrary, it is the only way of discarding dualism. Manicheism, or strict dualism, supposes the existence at the same time of two God-like Beings, equally infinite, powerful, and who are opposed to each other. The Christian belief, as exposed above, does not leave an inch of ground on which this doctrine could rest, since it supposes that *good* alone exists, and *evil* is simply its limitation. Mr. Mill, on the contrary, expresses his great displeasure at Christianity, or rather theism, because he thinks that evil exists, and he makes God responsible for it. He thus becomes himself a Manichean by grumbling against the existence of evil and expressing his impotent wish that it might cease. But this discussion, in good conscience, is already too long. We must return to the state of war.

Was it war, in fact? All our descriptions seemed to insinuate it, for the object was to portray humanity under the type of diminutive birds; and every one must acknowledge that man is fond of war, and that for him there is almost uninterruptedly a state of war, undertaken occasionally for its own sake. But the reader has not forgotten the writer's declaration that the exterior facts in this story can be relied upon, because they have happened exactly as they are represented; but as to the motives assigned to the birds in this book, they must be taken for what they are worth, and their truth cannot be altogether vouched for. The fact is that, at least in our opinion, there is on earth a real state of war for men only, who often have other motives than their whims for indulging in it. But with animals the case is altogether different. What appears amongst them to be war is simply the result of their position in nature. Many of them must eat flesh in order to live, and they cannot help it. As soon as their appetite is satisfied they cease from war; and the lion himself, when he is full, never attacks any prey.

I must consequently confess that I have made the Twit-Twats, and even the native birds, more ferocious than they really are. But it was the necessity of the case that obliged me to do so. I had to represent mankind under the veil of an allegory; and who does not know the irrepressible inclination for bloodshed which is every day witnessed among us? It shows itself in every possible form: feuds in private families, open rupture of former friendship, deep hatred of old enemies, brawls in taverns, the famous word, *Stand and deliver!* on the highways, the madness of the inebriate, the fury of lust, the greed of avarice, all the other passions that sway the human heart, end frequently in blood, and the papers we read every day are often merely catalogues of similar tragedies.

This, however, is entirely the result of *individual* excesses produced by human passions. What could not be said of the fearful doings of *nations* in the same line? When millions of men are arrayed against each other and come to blows, with their monstrous engines of war and their ingenious devices for destroying life, then the earth shakes, and the sun is obscured, and the moon refuses her light, and Nature seems to be hastening to her end.

Pages of a similar import could be written. We prefer to come to a more direct justification of our poor friends the Twit-Twats. Read their history again, as it has been so far described, and you will be inclined either to admit their perfect innocence, or at all events to believe them guilty of a slight misdemeanor. Were they not constantly acting in self-defence? And this is a sufficient excuse, as every one knows. Once, it is true, we have felt compelled to pronounce them in appearance to be *aggressors* and *invaders* of their antagonists' territory. But although we could not then divine their precise motives, some were suggested sufficient even for a rigorous moralist. And on all those most satisfactory reasons our cause rests with the public—that is, with those who take interest in this story. They will concede, it is to be hoped, that the main drift of it is promotive of virtue and good feeling. This chapter may seem to be an anomaly, and to be intended for fostering in the reader's heart a fierce martial ardor which the Christian cannot but deprecate. If it were so it would be going in a direction altogether contrary to the main tenor of the book. But it can be easily understood that this is only an appearance; and as the matter has been sifted, even metaphysically, to the bottom, no one now has a right to assert that the Twit-Twats were at any moment of their checkered life swaggerers, fire-eaters, bullies, braggadocios, or jackanapes. Their unpretending history will never expose the unsophisticated reader to the danger of contracting such frightfully bad habits, or rather such downright vices which could not but lead to depravity.

CHAPTER VIII.

SUSPENSION OF HOSTILITIES—MATING OF THE BIRDS—BUILDING OF THEIR NESTS.

THE last chapter left both foreign and native birds in a somewhat disordered condition. If there appears something confused about their existence since the Christmas day previous, it is owing entirely to my desire to be brief in my descriptions. But Horace himself long ago furnished me a good excuse, for he says in his *Ars Poetica:* "If you wish to be concise there is danger of becoming obscure." Yet even if the reader has easily followed the drift of the story so far, a few words more will make it clearer. The natives, settled at the very beginning on the roofs of the church and parsonage and in the row of poplar-trees, had finally changed places with the Twit-Twats, who had at first occupied the front of the sisters' convent, but not their garden. The native clan, dissatisfied probably with their patriarch, on the great day of the Saviour's birth had gradually left their quarters, to my great surprise, and had at last invaded the sisters' garden as well as the front of the convent, where they found the Twit-Twats in force; and this, together perhaps with the fight for *screenings*, was the origin, if not the immediate cause, of the war that has been described.

When the struggle was over the Irish birds were in possession of the whole convent territory as well as of the church and parsonage. They were, in fact, conquerors of a large empire, to which they would certainly not have dared to raise their aspirations before the first native attack.

The latter wretched birds, though altogether routed from between Third and Second Streets and forced to move toward the west, had not, however, been driven into the Hudson River. Their first care was to reorganize their battalions before the coming of the gentle spring. This they did by settling in the wide district in which they found themselves after the battle. It happened, fortunately for them, that there was not as yet a single sparrow established in that quarter. They could rest and recruit themselves, and many warriors of their tribe, who had been supposed slain on the battle-field among that "hecatomb" of victims of which I spoke, came back, one after another, like the stragglers spoken of constantly in the histories of war among men. It turned out, in fact, that their dead were comparatively few, and thus their ranks were, after all, not greatly diminished. It took, however, the whole of February and March to bring the natives to that consoling view of their position and to reanimate them with a new courage.

They soon sent out scouts toward their old quarters, and began to reoccupy some of their former positions along Third Street, but not as yet in any of the famous Lombardy poplars. The Twit-Twats, who witnessed these movements, did not, perhaps, sufficiently reflect on the possible consequences; but as they had full possession of the convent and indefinite elbow—or wing—room in an eastern direction, perhaps they thought it unnecessary to show irritation. Such was the position of both parties when April arrived. It was, in fact, a *suspension of hostilities.*

It is proper to say a word again of the primitive bird-cottage. Old General Twit-Twat and his Amazon had not left it, and they continued to live in great concord with both the native patriarchs. These two venerable birds appeared to feel no regret for the discomfiture and departure of their turbulent progeny. I often saw them early in the morning or late in the afternoon near the door of their own cell, generally one outside and the other inside of the cottage, only their heads being visible from my room. Sometimes the old Twit-Twats were at the same moment resting near the entrance to their own cell, and I felt a sensible pleasure in closely examining the four old creatures forming one group, as it were *en famille,* resting on their little feet, basking in the rays of the setting sun, looking gently at each other, or even softly chattering as if they were engaged in rational conversation. Such a scene would have been sufficient to inspire a poet; but I was too lazy at the time to write in verse, and I contented myself with looking and making a note of it.

Meanwhile spring came on. The Lombardy poplars were almost green, and the sweet odor exhaling from their expanding buds filled the rooms of the rectory (when the windows were opened) as if a whole establishment of cosmetics had been set up by the enterprising sparrows for the especial purpose of gently tickling my olfactory nerves. I was resting one day near one of the windows, inhaling the delicious perfume, when all at once I perceived better than ever before the sudden and irresistible advance of gentle spring. The maple-trees and elms planted along our side of Third Street were just opening their clusters of blossoms, which are generally despised by the ignorant, but produce on the learned in botany a feeling of surprise and admiration; the lilac bushes in the small gardens around were bursting with the inevitable propensity of showing off their young leaves and their pyramids of flower-buds; a few daffodils were not afraid of exposing to the blasts of fickle April their yellow corollas, so well protected until this moment.

This evident progress among flowering shrubs and trees was due to a few days of a mild temperature and a genial breeze. The air was balmy and the snow had quite disappeared; the few light and fleecy clouds in the blue sky announced beyond a doubt that they were no longer loaded with sleet and hail, but carried gentle dew and warm rain. The sun was now bright, and not only was its genial influence felt in the whole atmosphere and on the surface of ponds and rivers, but even the crust of the soil, the bark of trees, the skin of man, and the thick, downy covering of birds and lambs became all at once, as it were, conscious of it. It was spring indeed, and the whole little world of the sparrows was soon going to be a sort of primitive paradise. The patriarchs in both cells in the bird-cottage felt it in spite of their advanced age, and I perceived at this moment all four of them standing with evident delight on their diminutive platform, *twitting* and *twaiting*—let the reader allow me at least the liberty of coining these words—through the opening leaves of their budding poplar-tree. Whenever a gust of warm wind separated the branches for a moment the glorious orb of day touched them with its beams, and they fluttered with glee on feeling the gentle warmth of its rays.

It was time, I thought, for the sparrows to mate and begin building their nests; but on a sudden I found that sparrows' perceptions were keener than mine. The birds had been at it for several days, and I was ignorant of it. Man often imagines that because he is the "lord of creation" he could actively rule it, and could supervise all the operations recorded in the *Opera et Dies* of Hesiod. The world would be sadly governed indeed if this pretension were to be carried out. Many animated beings besides the sparrows would remain much behind in their calculations, if they had to wait for the order of their master, proud man. But fortunately man's rights over nature are not strictly protected, and his humble servants, the mere animals, often take upon themselves to act without waiting for his commands. On the present occasion, though I could consider myself the master of this little world, in which I took the liveliest interest, the birds did very well not to remain idle until I spoke, for they had already done a great deal of which I must inform the reader, and upon which I had not the least influence.

I cannot say if they had begun their mating exactly on St. Valentine's day, which always falls on February 14, which was more than a month before I perceived the arrival of spring. The story of the holy martyr St. Valentine is well known, and there is, after all, nothing impossible for a great saint in the most difficult task which is assigned to him by the legend—namely, that of presiding at all matrimonial alliances in the birds' republic. But the Church has left everybody free to have his own opinion on the subject.

Not having been sufficiently on the watch, I cannot exactly say if all the sparrows were mated as early as February 14. But I can vouch that on the day when my eyes were suddenly opened, whose exact date I cannot now furnish, but which was undoubtedly very early in April—not later than the 8th—the male sparrows were all in the happy condition of benedicts. They had already selected their place of dwelling for the summer, and some of them had begun their nests. These various operations require of me some details, and my long observation of the whole process enables me to speak almost *ex professo*.

The reader must know first that there is seldom any fighting for the best localities, although there is undoubtedly a great difference between the various nooks and corners and holes among which the sparrows have to choose. Some of these places are most convenient, others most unsuitable and objectionable; and as each sparrow couple looks first for itself, it would be natural to suppose there would be no end of wrangling and contention among them on so important a subject. Suppose that the United States government had not arranged its pre-emption laws as prudently as it has done, and had allowed all new settlers to decide for themselves the question of *locating* their claims; what a nice state of affairs we should have among the border ruffians, as some of the frontiersmen used to be called! But the sparrows, without any State or Federal legislatures, have succeeded in deciding all these primitive questions of property in the simplest and most peaceful manner. I do not know if there is any such thing as a *contrat social* for them, as Rousseau thought there was, or must be, for mankind; but it looks as if there had been an agreement among all the individuals composing sparrowdom that the first occupant of any locality should have a sacred right to its possession, and (what is still better) as if all sparrows, without exception, were most faithful as to the inviolate keeping of that agreement. If you are on the lookout in early spring, when this interesting operation is taking place, you will before long remark that in case a fine pair of birds, evidently just arrived from another State, happen to alight at the entrance to a hole which they had descried from a great distance and had imagined to be precisely what they wanted, as soon as they perceive it to be already occupied by another couple they retire with great modesty and prudence to look for another place. They do not show a desire to take forcible possession; and indeed they carry their peaceful demeanor so far as to manifest the same good nature even when there is no prospect of finding another place, and they see themselves compelled to build the awkward nests of which we shall speak by and by, and which are their last makeshift. This is certainly remarkable in birds that are so boisterous, and I must confess that in this regard the native sparrows were no worse than the Twit-Twats.

It will not do here to enter into a protracted disquisition on the interesting subject of nest-building among birds. The nests of sparrows are the only ones that can be examined at this moment. Such as we know them, sparrows are almost half-domesticated animals; and it is known that all creatures of that description depending more or less on man show very little skill in anything connected with their domestic economy. Look at animals that are altogether under man's control, and say if they do not appear altogether stupid. The hen, for instance, the goose, the canary-bird even, no more know how to construct a nest than they do how to regulate for themselves the number of their eggs and the frequency of their broods. It would be unfair, therefore, to expect sparrows to be skilful mechanics or artistic builders. Among them are no weavers, no carpenters, no wood-sawyers, no masons, not, in fine, any artificers whatever—unlike many free-winged tribes whose splendid works of all those kinds are described in books of natural history.

The sparrows' only skill consists in selecting a hole and stuffing it with hay, or dried grass, or even bits of paper or threads of wool and cotton; all this spread at random,

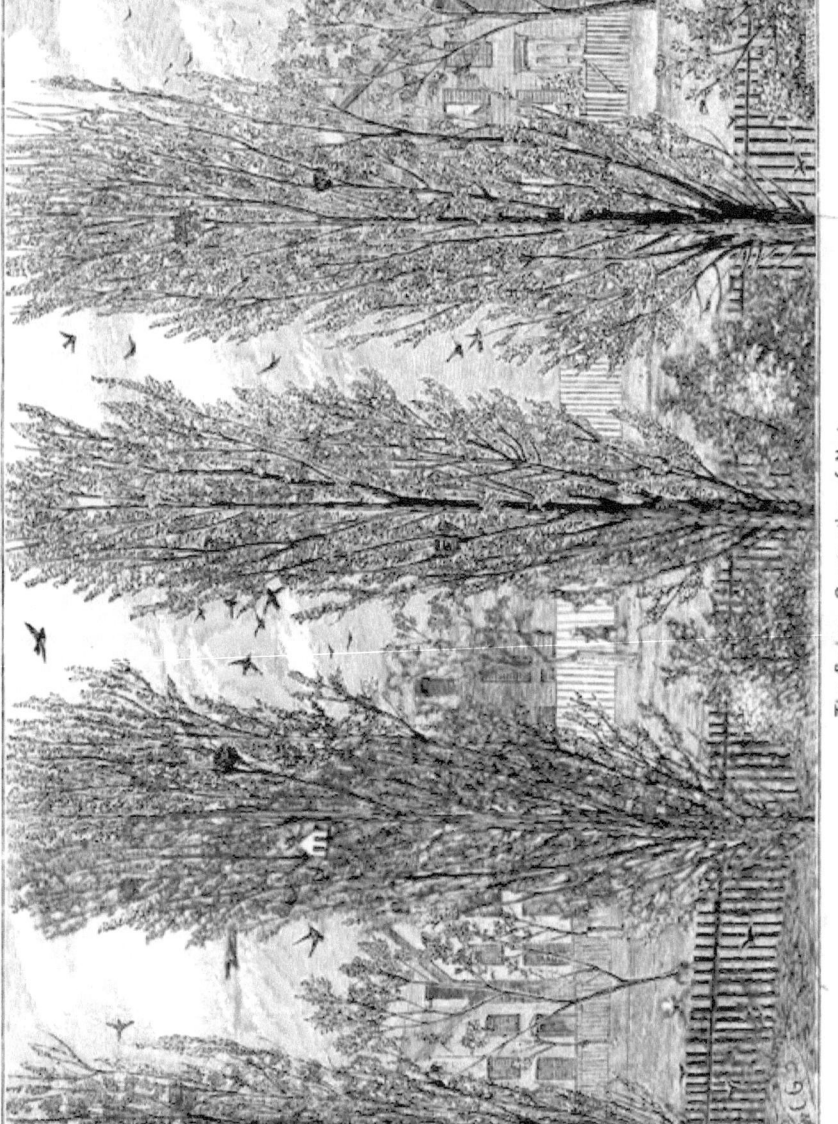

The Spring—Construction of Nests.

with an eye more to bulk than to perfection of details. They depend so much on man for helping them to procure even these clumsy materials that if you have the kindness to spread before your door all the sweepings of your rooms they will appear very thankful. Should you happen to be a milliner your neighborhood will be for them a place of predilection; and of all the refuse of your workshop—silk, cotton, wool, straw, etc., etc.—they will make a clean sweep, leaving on the ground only the pins and the needles which they do not appear to need, and of which they have not as yet learned the various uses. Nay, more, should you wish to gratify them completely and make them at once your friends, follow exactly the prescription I am going to give you, and which my personal experience when a boy has proved to me to be the best. Take a good-sized earthen crock, and make a round hole in the bottom of it large enough for the birds to enter; hang it to a nail near some back window, visible only from a yard where the sparrows venture to come. Fill the vessel with hay and some clean rags, and see chiefly that its large mouth is nailed tightly against the house wall. The couple of sparrows that will see it first will be in an ecstasy of delight at a godsend which delivers them from the trouble of finding a hole and building a nest. They will probably be there the morning after you have hung up the crock; in a few days, at the latest, there will be some eggs in it, and at the end of a few weeks you will have a brood of five or six new-fledged sparrows, of whom you can dispose as you choose. This shows better than anything else the habits of these birds with respect to nest-building.

But now back to our narrative. Soon all around the rectory, the church, and the convent the Twit-Twats were busy attending to their domestic concerns. As I did not wish them to acquire habits of complete laziness, I took good care not to furnish them with crocks and pots. They had to look for places of refuge, and to display their industry in garnishing them the best way they could. There were no holes in the walls, as all the buildings around were new, or nearly so; but there were many recesses, cornices, projecting eaves, and angles of every description. The reader already knows that the front of the convent was full of such things as these, and that in November and December there were reasons why they would not be comfortable for birds. But in early April the poor sparrows were not wise enough to foresee anything of the kind, and some of them selected with avidity spots which, at the end of the breeding season, they would find to their cost would be far from pleasant.

It was a pleasure, nevertheless, to see them at work. They flew from every quarter and went in all directions. I have seen some of them carry in their comparatively slender bills long shreds of every possible sort of materials, though hay and straw predominated. It would be curious, as we have hinted before, to empty their holes in the fall and examine with care the stuff of which the beds of their young are composed. A systematic statistician would find there an interesting subject of study, more useful, perhaps, than many of the usual attempts at moral, physical, and philosophical speculations from statistics.

One great advantage resulted from their well-meant activity—they did not think of fighting. The dreadful tragedies which have been sufficiently portrayed always happen late in the season and chiefly in the heart of winter. When they think exclusively of the birth and the rearing of their young their breasts are animated only with soft feelings, and the quiet domestic virtues reign supreme among them. Their moral condition is in accord with the gentle breathing of the air around; and though they are never heard to coo like the doves, I have no doubt that they are under the same mollifying influence, but are unable to express it by their throats, owing altogether to the difference of organization. Be this as it may, the golden age had certainly come back for them, and their extensive empire looked like a paradise of innocence and guiltlessness. All this, it is to be remarked, happened in the Twit-Twats' dominion only, for they were complete masters of this new Garden of Eden.

Meanwhile what were the conquered natives doing? This is an important question for the progress of the story. Had they entirely given up their guilty plots, and was there not some danger to be expected from that quarter? It has been seen that in the new district where they had settled they had found no other sparrows, and thus could indulge in strife among themselves only. The severe punishment, moreover, which they had received had somewhat cooled their martial ardor, and it was to be hoped that, for some time at least, they would keep the peace. It has been remarked, however, that they had already sent out scouts in the direction of their former grounds, and had reoccupied some of their old positions along Third Street, but on the western side of it. Along that line of manœuvre they were in a dangerous proximity to the Twit-Twat possessions; but as they also appeared to be altogether occupied with nest-building, there was a possibility that there would be no conflict.

Unfortunately the peculiarity of their position to a great degree curtailed their chances of an indefinite multiplication by breeding. In their new territory they had found no edifice of large proportions—no churches, no convents, no parsonages. Only far toward the west and north there were huge iron-factories looming up along the Hudson River; but the constant noise, the dense smoke, the brightness of a lurid fire which issued forth from windows and doors, instead of inviting them to come, were calculated to fill them with terror. The houses in the midst of which they had settled were all very small—only one or two stories high—and offered to the sight no cornices, no recesses, no angles whatever. To complete the despairing look of the situation, no trees had been planted along the streets, and you could see in the little gardens back of the houses only an abundance of potatoes and cabbages, and perhaps a few shrubs of the most humble and common kind where sparrows never think of nestling. The prospect of the natives, it must be confessed, was disheartening.

Some of them had already begun their nests under the far-projecting eaves of a public school-house, which was the only prominent object along Second Street; but this edifice, though roomy and somewhat imposing, was not large enough by far for the conquered tribe, so that the problem appeared indeed insoluble, as they say in algebra. Many of them went as far as a solitary old farm-house which still stood on the bank of the river at the very extreme southwestern limit of the new native territory. But besides several ugly dogs and cats which were always prowling around that desolate spot, there were no less than four families living in the house, all, as usual, blessed with a number of children, for whom the sparrows feel an excusable aversion. In spite of all these disadvantages, that dingy old dwelling was soon honeycombed with nests, preparatory to containing a large colony of young birds, destined most of them to death under the teeth of dogs and cats, or to slavery in the hands of unfeeling boys.

In these circumstances many of the natives, unable to find accommodation in their undisputed district, began to crowd on the side of it nearest to the Twit-Twat empire, since it has been justly so called. Many of them, however, keeping strictly to their own side of Third Street, and pushing north, fortunately found better houses as well as a row of large trees planted many years back, where they immediately began to build nests, as there were not holes and corners enough around. There remained at last only half a dozen native couples still unprovided, and they placed themselves on guard just in front of the Lombardy poplars, where they had thrived for so long a time, and whither some of them were evidently bent on returning. They thought probably that, since their patriarchal sires were still living in the little cottage which they shared so amicably with old General Twit-Twat and his Amazon, they also had a right to occupy any vacant spot in the neighborhood. This was ominous of future contention.

I eagerly followed with my eyes the doings of this bold colony, from which I foresaw that the evils of war might again ensue. A very remarkable fact confirmed me in my former opinion about the *sacredness* of the rights vested in the first occupants of holes and recesses. All these were tenanted by Twit-Twat couples, and no native dared to disturb them in their possession. Though the same antipathy evidently continued to exist between both races, none of the defeated birds appeared inclined even to controvert the rights of their natural enemies and endeavor to drive them off by force from their peaceful abodes. Their only object was to build nests of their own in the tall poplars so often mentioned, which were then a part and parcel of the Twit-Twat empire.

Soon a bold native pair flew up to the very top of one of the largest trees and began furiously to chirp, as if they were daring any opponent to evict them. This proceeding was directly imitated by the five other unprovided couples; and I then understood that we were probably going to enjoy the sight of six huge nests, whose building-up I would be able to study with the greatest advantage. In fact, the first pair that had arrived began operations immediately on taking possession of the tree.

The poplar they had selected was at some distance from the windows of my room, and had grown to larger proportions than many of the others, on account of the rich soil its roots had found by a lucky chance. At a distance of about fifteen feet from the ground a strong limb grew from the trunk, surrounded at the junction by a number of small shoots forming a kind of loose wicker basket close to the tree and adorned with green leaves, around which, most of the time, a gentle breeze seemed to play wantonly.

The two birds, not losing a moment's time (for April was already on the wane, and all the other pairs were ahead of them), pounced upon everything they could find in the street, and brought to the spot they had chosen either long strings of hay and straw that had fallen from farmers' carts, or narrow strips of blue, red, or white paper carried by the wind from the houses and scattered without order in all directions. There could not, indeed, be observed in their work the same regularity as in the nest of the European goldfinch, or, better still, in that of the Baltimore oriole. The sparrows, as was said, are wretched architects and make very poor weavers. They answer among birds to the race of troglodytes among men, who, according to modern ethnologists, lived originally in caves before our species had the skill of inventing dwellings of wood or stone. I must again repeat that when the sparrows cannot possibly find any hole or natural recess in walls or rocks they are compelled to roughly build in the branches of trees ugly apologies for nests, which have nothing in common with the airy constructions of chaffinches or black-caps. Their attempts at architecture or weaving result in sorry specimens of unsightly ugliness and absolute deformity. You can see among the green leaves only a shapeless mass, or rather an ill-looking heap of incougruous materials, against which the wind will howl and the rain pour in torrents, in order promptly to demolish it, when the stormy season of November arrives. This was the sorry sight afforded by the active and untiring natives in their awkward building operations.

I was, however, anxious to discover if there were not some redeeming features in their fantastic work, as I could not believe that these industrious birds were altogether deprived of skill and ingenuity. I wished to better judge of their ability to procure interior comfort, at least, if they were far from remarkable for the exterior beauty of their dwellings. I could not think, at my age, of risking my life on a rough ladder, which was at hand and could be placed against the slender trunk of the poplar-tree. But on the very top of the rectory there was, fortunately, and there is still, a square platform surrounded by white banisters, from which, with the help of my opera-glass, I could easily distinguish the whole interior of this last refuge of the poor defeated birds. I soon became almost lost in surprise and admiration. Had they finished their nest above by constructing a large aperture open to heaven, as is the custom for many birds, it would have naturally ended below in something like the inverted tube of a funnel, and thus their young would have been at the mercy of cold, wind, and rain, and exposed to all the fury of April storms. They had shown a great deal of good sense, for they gave it, on the contrary, a quite different shape. On the side looking south they had intertwined their clumsy materials in the shape of a rude covered gallery, the opening receiving the sun's rays, and the lower end being the very bottom of the nest, eight inches at least from the aperture.

THE TWIT-TWATS.

From the high platform where I stood a good part of the city of Troy could be seen, but I confess that at this moment my attention was altogether engrossed by the single object hanging like a misshapen wisp of straw thrown at random against the stem of a poplar-tree. This was sufficient, in my mind, to redeem the wrongly-despised judgment of my dear sparrows.

There is no need of repeating the same lengthened narrative for the five other pairs of birds who had remained unaccommodated with a place for rearing their young. They constructed their nests in the same fashion, and I had a splendid opportunity of observing their ways of acting when they have a nest as well as when they have a hole. My leisure time during the month of April was devoted to that study.

I shall not annoy the reader with the tedious recital of all my discoveries, which were most of them of little consequence for others, though they were all full of interest for me. But a remarkable fact resulting from all that nest-building, and of great importance for the sequel of this story, cannot be left altogether unrecorded, the more so that it gave increased boldness to the whole native crew and became the source of manifold miseries to the Twit-Twats. It would have been a great blessing for both races had the strict separation continued which was the happy result of the bloody war described in the last chapter. But the near neighborhood of the wandering birds in the poplar-trees, and the actual presence of the venerable native couple, who continued to live peacefully in the midst of the victorious Twit-Twats, were the fatal occasion which brought in their train new misfortunes to our interesting little friends.

CHAPTER IX.

OMINOUS RISING OF A NEW NATIVE LEADER—MULTIPLICATION OF BOTH RACES.

HE first bold bird who constructed his awkward nest in the renowned poplar-tree was undoubtedly the oldest and most famous of all the progeny of the ancient native patriarchs. I had remarked him very many times before. He had taken a most active part in the battles that had well-nigh destroyed the Twit-Twat race in and around the sisters' convent. I would easily have distinguished him among a thousand other sparrows; but there was particularly an honorable scar left on his face in one of the most furious contests of the previous winter's campaign —a scar which must be described in detail, in order to show that the identity of the bird cannot be controverted.

Everybody knows that around, and chiefly at the base of, the stiff bill which adorns the anterior part of the head of all sparrows there are rudiments of feathers, which are, perhaps, more ornamental than useful, though naturalists cannot say that they are altogether without utility. I have just said that they are *rudiments* of feathers, because, in fact, of ordinary bird-coverings they have the ribs only, and the bright appendages on either side of the middle rib are totally wanting. These adjuncts to the sparrow's bill could be called *bristles* rather than feathers; but we prefer entirely to discard that word as manifestly unworthy the young hero of whom we now speak. But he shared in great part in the misfortune of Samson Agonistes. In one of the fiercest engagements of the late war an infuriated Twit-Twat, under the influence of intense rage, had pounced upon young Mr. Native, and, holding him firmly on the ground under both his claws, had furiously pecked at these appendages of his enemy, and had made a clean sweep of them all. And as young Twit-Twat had, in his hate, extracted the very roots of these bill-ornaments, they could not be renewed, and for all his life the unfortunate young native was destined to have his name written on his face. For this simple reason I repeat again that I could easily distinguish him from a thousand others.

When his nest was finally constructed several days passed, as usual for all birds, before his hen began to deposit her eggs and hatch them. During this short period of idleness he had nothing better to do than to examine his surroundings and become acquainted by sight with everything of note in his neighborhood. He then became sorrowfully aware that there were more enemies than friends in his present locality. There was, however, a great exception, since his tree was not far distant from the one which contained the patriarchs' cottage, and he knew that his very father lived in one of the two cells. I do not know if there was still some filial piety lingering in his heart, of which he had not certainly given any proof for a very long time; but whatever may have been his motive, he one day flew away from the top of his poplar, and alighted just on the platform where at that very moment old Mr. Native was resting alone, for his sweet companion was bent with age and at that time was sick in the interior of her own cell.

When the young bird came into the presence of his ancient sire he seemed respectful enough, so far as a studied reserve can be called "respect." Still, the venerable patriarch did not appear to trust him completely, and, making one or two steps in advance as a kind of trial, he seemed to say: "I am here a hermit for you; what news do you bring me of the family?" The young bird did not appear insulted at that kind of reproach. He even modestly withdrew from before the steps of his advancing father; and, both showing themselves more reconciled, they flew up a short distance without leaving the tree, and rested on two different branches, very near each other, yet demurely keeping their distance. They did not at first change their position, nor did they become familiar enough to perch on the same twig and gently peck at each other, as sparrows generally do. Thus they stood facing each other for about a quarter of an hour; and I confess it would have been particularly interesting to me to know what they *said* to each other. I have scarcely any doubt that animals often understand each other and have a peculiar way of *speaking* without uttering a word, for they cannot have an articulate language; that seems naturally to follow the possession of reason.

At the end of the *conversation* there appeared to be a far greater degree of good feeling, and they hopped alternately from one branch to another in evident play, as if they were on terms of familiarity such as I had not witnessed among them for a very long time indeed.

There might not have been very serious consequences for the Twit-Twats from this first interview between *father and son* had the new-born intimacy been limited to that single pair; but the other native birds of the neighborhood, particularly those who were at the time engaged in building their nests, had remarked it, and soon we shall have to record the first growling of another storm more pregnant with evil to the native race than the first one, and which will keep the poor Twit-Twats likewise in hot water until their final triumph, unfortunately delayed by the turbulence of their enemies.

The native crew, emboldened by the example of their scarred young leader, came one after another to have a look at their patriarch. He received them with a cautious demeanor, but did not drive them away. They gradually grew more familiar and arrived in greater number, so as to cover the little platform, and even some of the branches around the bird-cottage. What they said, or whether they said anything, I cannot positively tell, for there was always some boisterousness in their manner which prevented me from paying great attention to their *speaking* organs. But, unless it was the effect of prejudice on my part, I never could detect the same familiarity of intercourse between the native brood and their old sire which always appeared whenever some of the Twit-Twat progeny came into the presence of their old general and his Amazon. The natives invariably showed a harshness of disposition akin to positive animosity; and although the gloomy and violent young birds seemed in a sort of constraint and awe when in the presence of their ancient parent, although they went so far as to pay him a kind of deference—by getting out of his way, for instance, when the question was who should pass before the other—still the contrast between their conduct and that of the young Twit-Twats in the same circumstances was so striking that I was sometimes tempted to suppose they belonged to radically different species of birds.

Meanwhile the Twit-Twats swarming about had observed with suspicion these strange doings, and began to fear for the consequences of such a bold step on the part of their adversaries. They did not, however, show any disposition to fight, but, with a great deal of cunning, they evidently formed the counter project of improvising a public demonstration on their side in honor of their chief, as a set-off to that of the opposite quarter. They came, therefore, in crowds; for they now enjoyed, particularly in and around the Lombardy poplars, great superiority of number over their enemies. Still, they did not seem to come for the purpose of provoking a quarrel, but only in order to gladden the heart of their old parent by the sight of their frisky gambols. They hopped, skipped, and flew with perfect freedom, without minding in the least the invading natives. They seemed to know that they belonged to the household of old General Twit-Twat, or rather that his dwelling was the homestead of the whole family. They were friendly, gentle, attentive chiefly to the head of their sept; and I have seen on this occasion worms which they had brought in their little bills for feeding their young fall accidentally, as it were, in the way of the old bird, so that that dainty food could become his easy prey. It was delightful to contemplate the familiar relations they showed between father and sons. Particularly the sweet contrast between the amiable agility and rapidity of movement of youth on one side, and the graceful sedateness and natural gentleness of ripe age on the other, would have been, in my opinion, a most lovely subject for the brush of the painter or the fancy of the poet.

But the sight of this paradisiacal happiness could not but produce the most bitter and jealous feelings in the natives' hearts. I am confident that if their number had not been so inconsiderable war would have begun from this moment. They had to withdraw on account of being only a handful; and they appeared to do it modestly and naturally. But for ever after, whenever the natives came back to play the sycophants before their worthy chieftain, if there happened to be then only a few Twit-Twats around the cottage they immediately showed their deep hatred by their attitude, their gestures, their screams, and by the bristling of their feathers. They seemed to feel that they had finally found a leader.

There were even slight skirmishes now and then between the two camps, amounting almost to a declaration of hostility. On one occasion two natives were severely punished, and on another a poor Twit-Twat went away bleeding from the field. The two old patriarchs, however, both Twit-Twat and native, tried their best to allay the storm whenever it began to brew; for the reader knows that these two noble birds, at least, were inaccessible to petulance, rashness, and animosity, and that, had they been alone, peace would have continued to flourish, as it was meet and proper it should do, around the church and parsonage.

Besides the personal efforts of both chieftains, the breeding-time, now at its height, was likewise a great obstacle to war and strife. For we are now in April—pretty far down in the month—and each pair of birds has not only a nest, but a little offspring to protect and feed. And as to the care for their young I never could detect the smallest difference between American and Irish birds. The feeling of paternity, and chiefly maternity, is equal. It constantly asserts its power over the most ferocious natures as well as over the most gentle. Yes, let it be said in acknowledgment of the supreme rule of love which has been imposed by the Almighty Creator on all His works, vultures and eagles are as careful of their young and attentive to their wants as doves, even, or humming-birds can be. The cuckoo is the only one among birds who leaves his progeny to be fed by another; and on this account alone, if my personal opinion could have any weight among ornithologists, I should severely exclude the unfeeling fellow from a place in the gentle class of winged creatures, though his *coo-cooing* is so very pleasant in May.

Consequently, open war could not as yet break out among the sparrows in the Twit-Twat empire. Its fury was to be delayed until the end of the breeding-season, and even until the return of both clans from their *rustication* in summer. But directly after that epoch a state of affairs must inevitably prevail such as it has not yet been my sad duty to describe. For the seeds of contention were laid deep during the whole spring and summer which form the subject-matter of the actual part of our story. Meanwhile the sparrow species was multiplying to an enormous extent; and this requires a moment's attention, because an understanding of it will render possible to perceive the awful import of the final catastrophe.

Let the reader ponder over this simple, cool, and statistical statement: Each sparrow couple, in the course of a single summer, begets four and sometimes five broods, each one containing from four to six chicks. This, at least, is the result of my personal observation; and I give it without reference to what any book of natural history may say. With these simple data before you, calculate what will be the numbers of the two armies on their return from the usual *rustication*—say by the end of September. In reading the narrative of the previous winter's battles you have, perhaps, been surprised that so many birds could have come from two couples. Your astonishment will

Wonderful Increase among Sparrows.

be still greater when you see military operations carried on by solid troops twenty or twenty-five times larger again. For mark it well, all active Twit-Twats and natives are now very busy increasing their numbers in what is called a more than *geometrical ratio*. You know what this means, if you have ever got far along in arithmetic. Should you have neglected it in your childhood the importance of the present subject requires that you should take it up at once, if possible, even at this late period of your life. In the meantime I shall leave you buried in that interesting occupation.

But no, wait a moment. I have been somewhat inexact in saying that all the sparrow couples were obeying a great law of their nature and following God's command to increase and multiply. There were two pairs which had absolutely nothing to do, except to keep the general peace and see to the interests of order. These were no others than the old patriarchs of both races. No new progeny was ever to issue forth from the two contiguous cells of their cottage. In their old age they were not to be troubled with the care of feeding successively during the summer twenty or twenty-five voracious mouths, such as you must often have seen if you have looked at birds' nests containing the young ones. If you wish to have a better idea of this trouble of the birds than you have probably ever had before, procure a nest of unfledged woodpeckers, as fell once to my lot, and try to feed them yourself. Only in this way will you be able to judge. The venerable sires of all our sparrows were to be at last exempt from that labor, and would have to feed themselves only. Consequently, for the sake of perfect exactness, I advise you, in the arithmetical calculation which I have suggested, not to include these two noble pairs, which must, however, continue to remain the most conspicuous actors on our stage until the end of the story.

This chapter in its entirety is devoted to the illustration of the unfortunate position in which immigrants to this country, especially Catholics, find themselves on many occasions. They can scarcely escape contention, and, though they may be perfectly innocent of giving any cause of quarrel, the strife will nevertheless be attributed to them. This is chiefly owing to those un-American factions which occasionally arise under the pretext of protecting *natives* against *foreigners*. These factions are called here un-American because their scope is entirely opposed to the genuine spirit of this republic. All its citizens enjoy equal rights under the Constitution, and to make antagonistic classes of them is to go counter to the spirit of true Americanism. All in this country have been originally foreigners, and if some of its citizens are happy enough to have for a long time enjoyed its privileges, those who have but lately arrived know that their children and grandchildren will be in the same position; and meanwhile, as soon as they have fulfilled all the conditions imposed by the naturalization laws, they have a right to claim and enjoy the advantages of full citizenship.

But what is chiefly intended in this chapter is to describe a large number of warmhearted Americans who, born in this country and knowing that the residence of their family on these shores dates from early colonial times, still not only refuse to espouse the *native* cause as proposed by newly-organized native factions, but show themselves friends and supporters of those who are unjustly called foreigners and aliens even after they have honestly fulfilled all the provisions of the law with regard to citizenship.

In this chapter, it is true, this class of fair-minded—nay, generous—men is represented by one single pair of patriarchs only among the birds, but this noble pair are the representatives of a class very numerous in this country. Every one of us, I am sure, is acquainted with many such, and I could relate stories without end showing that the American people are in general not only fair-minded and warm-hearted, as I called them, but ready at all times to help by their efforts and their means the poorest immigrant, landed only yesterday at Castle Garden, who falls casually in their way.

These are the true *natives* of this country, and they alone know and appreciate the true spirit of its institutions. And these brief hints will show how well connected is the web of our tale, which it is time to resume.

CHAPTER X.

THE SPARROWS' RUSTICATION ENDED BY AN EVENTFUL CATASTROPHE—RETURN OF THE BIRDS.

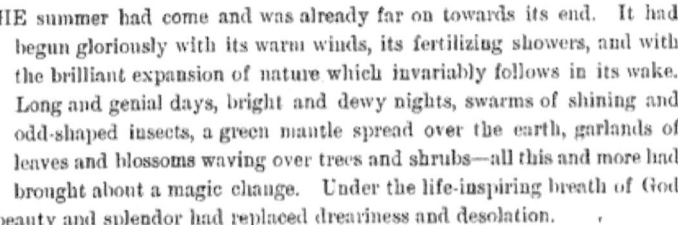

THE summer had come and was already far on towards its end. It had begun gloriously with its warm winds, its fertilizing showers, and with the brilliant expansion of nature which invariably follows in its wake. Long and genial days, bright and dewy nights, swarms of shining and odd-shaped insects, a green mantle spread over the earth, garlands of leaves and blossoms waving over trees and shrubs—all this and more had brought about a magic change. Under the life-inspiring breath of God beauty and splendor had replaced dreariness and desolation.

The sparrows were most of the time hidden under a rich canopy of boughs; the poplars were, in fact, green pyramids of moving velvet, gracefully rocking at the slightest breath of air. But you could hear the twittering of the birds and see them suddenly emerging from under the ample folds of bright draperies as they flew after one another, dancing, as it were, in circles around the tall and slender trees.

The unshapely objects which you could have seen during winter from my window—the trunks, the limbs, the old stumps, the twigs even and branchlets—were no longer in view; everything misshapen and distorted had been artfully concealed by the great Author of all beauty and gracefulness. But the little platform of the double sparrow-cottage so frequently mentioned was still in full view, and the ancient Twit-Twats, as well as their old native neighbors, often graced it by their presence. They constantly came out and went in, but no young brood was ever seen to issue from either door. The old birds nevertheless seemed happy, and no doubt enjoyed themselves very much. They were oftentimes visited by the numerous young sparrows nestled all around—those from Irish quarters more lively and sociable than ever, the others apparently more courteous and respectful toward the patriarch of their tribe, though they still kept up a grudge against the unoffending Twit-Twats. This, it has been seen, occasionally broke out in squabbles, and during the whole summer there were now and then hostile engagements, which nevertheless did not bring on a state of open war. Altogether it appeared as if affairs went on very much as they have done with birds since the beginning of creation.

The ancient male native appeared at times rather gloomy, and occasionally he would stand motionless for more than a quarter of an hour on the little platform of his cottage, seemingly immersed in thought. On these occasions the younger bird with the remarkable scar, whom I had previously ascertained to be his first and oldest surviving offspring, would invariably perch near him, and the interview always produced a visible change for the better in the old bird.

These were the chief incidents of the summer. Autumn alone could bring about any remarkable change in the situation. Suddenly all the sparrows disappeared. Young and old, lately fledged birds of this summer as well as ancient stagers of eight or ten years, all took their flight without having given any previous notice, as if they had agreed among themselves to abandon this part of the country and go no one knew whither.

I have studied sparrowdom from my early youth, and very long ago, in the Old World, I had remarked that after the usual summer increase the families formed in large groups and went rambling together for several weeks; but I had never before been so forcibly struck by this curious phenomenon, and the circumstances attending it now were so strange that at first I thought the birds had gone for good and would never return.

For it was not a migration to a milder climate—something the sparrows never need, since they are the only birds in this country which can stand our severe northern winters. Besides, even had this been their object it was still too early, as it was only the end of August and the weather was oppressively hot. They could not have been in need of a warmer country. Besides, they had taken none of the precautions which birds generally take when migrating at the beginning of winter—that is, they had not appointed leaders and watchmen over their flight, as ducks, geese, and starlings do; they had not started together in good order and with any foresight against possible danger; they had simply dispersed and disappeared. It was very strange. As it was during daylight that it happened, I witnessed it all, and it was something I could not understand.

Would my birds ever return? That was the question. Three years before in another locality I had seen other sparrows depart and return; and in order to treat the subject scientifically, as is ever my wont, I must give the details of that other remarkable story, which appeared to me to differ a great deal from the present one. I was then taking care of a congregation in Jersey City, on the celebrated Heights, not far from Bergen, and very near what is called Palisade Avenue. The church was large, built of stone, but not finished. The masons had not yet filled the holes which had been used for the scaffolding; there were hundreds of these holes, which were all full of sparrows when I went to live there. The birds were certainly more numerous in that place than they ever were around me in Troy; but I did not take so deep an interest in them, for I did not know their genealogy, and could not possibly have known it. There was in Jersey City no Irish Murrogh O'Murphy to acquaint me with the previous history of the broods, and consequently I did not give so much attention to the little fellows that hopped, skipped, and flew around St. Joseph's Church in what was then called Hudson City. There were, however, birds enough, and I could not escape the infliction of their screams and the pleasurable sight of their gambols.

This lasted a good part of the summer, and in August they also went away in the unceremonious manner of my Trojans. I was told that it was usual with them to go off in this manner in August, and that they would return in September; they had merely gone into the country to enjoy themselves for a short time. And, in fact, before the last day of September they were all in their holes again. I began to have a faint notion that they had been *rusticating*, and this gave an additional interest to my subsequent studies of the subject.

But in Troy, when I enquired after their departure nobody could tell me as much about the matter as I knew myself. A circumstance which I learned afterwards explained the exact knowledge of the Jersey people and the complete ignorance of the Trojans. The first had, as was seen, received the sparrows from Europe long before New York, and in Hudson City they had already seen them at work for nearly ten years, and knew a great deal about their habits. The reader is aware that in South Troy the facts above related happened the year of the sparrows' first arrival, so that the ignorance of the people of Troy was perfectly excusable.

But I was somewhat perplexed. So far I had been highly favored in my studies concerning the sparrows' habits; but now, when everything appeared propitious, an unexpected turn had suddenly brought my studies to a close. Every circumstance of their flight seemed to indicate that they had gone for good—not only the reasons given a moment ago, derived from the want of order and preparation in the whole affair, but chiefly the terrible fights which had rendered the previous winter so disastrous for many of them. I myself had foreseen and feared it, and it is well known that birds of all classes are better able than man to foresee whatever is in store for them. Virgil has given strong proofs of it with regard to the Italian birds, particularly with regard to His Majesty the Woodpecker, a great *prophet*, according to the poet.

The thing was too important to be neglected. This period of the year, it is well known, is one of almost total leisure for clergymen. Many think they can absent themselves from their parishes and recruit, as they say, during a good part of a month, at the very least, provided provision is made that the sick are not left to die without the consolations of religion. I would not personally have dared, without good reasons and the usual authorization, to take so much liberty in a matter where conscience is so nearly concerned. But I could certainly roam at large within the precincts of my parish, and, since relaxation is necessary and at that season allowable, I thought the best relaxation for me would be to decide the most interesting and momentous question, What had become of my sparrows?

The first thing I did was to cross over from the rectory to Jackson Street, the next block south, and then, walking through Trenton Street along near the sisters' premises, I soon came in front of a dreary-looking quarry of blue-stone, over which I had often been obliged to climb, owing to the indentations in the rock made by the quarrymen. Then over the hill and through brushwood and stumps of cedar-trees I could push up until I reached the top. It was such a journey as Jonathan, the friend of young David, made when, accompanied by his armor-bearer only, "he sought to go over to the garrison of the Philistines, rocks standing up on both sides, and steep cliffs like *teeth* on one side and on the other" (1 Kings xiv. 4). This passage of Holy Scripture is a perfect description of the quarry situated at the east end of Trenton Street in Troy. All the Trojans know the place and can vouch for it. But I was on that day more peacefully inclined than Jonathan, and was merely looking for sparrows.

I soon found a great number of them. Some fields at a short distance had been sown with buckwheat, and, sure enough, here were birds very busy in the midst of the abundance of good things. But I could discover neither Twit-Twats nor any of my native birds among them, and my whole afternoon's labor was perfectly in vain. I wandered over that elevated plateau as far east as the poorhouse, and very far indeed south along the renowned Greenbush road, which does not, it must be said, lead you through *green bushes*. On all sides I saw sparrows feeding on the various kinds of seeds so common in autumn. But my pets were not to be seen, and if they had been in that neighborhood the reader knows I should easily have distinguished them from any other birds. I had, therefore, to return home somewhat tired and put out. Still, my rambles had convinced me that my poor friends were not altogether lost. It was evidently a custom of the race to leave their city habitations in the fall and take to the country for a while, for the sake of feeding better, as all my observations that day had given me the ocular demonstration.

After seriously reflecting for nearly half a week on the most probable places whither both Twit-Twats and natives could have gone, I thought of examining a locality very different from the previous one, and which enjoys many advantages over it. It is an extensive district just north of the one I had explored, and which, in fact, is the delightful little valley watered by the celebrated Poestenkill Creek in its upper course. A short description of its lower basin has been given at the very beginning of this story. A more complete one is in order here, because my efforts in that direction were to be successful.

The Poestenkill—this is, it seems, its Indian name, preserved to posterity by the Dutch when they settled in Rensselaer County—runs irregularly from east to west through a hilly district which appears to be a spur of the Heidelberg Mountains. In winter the creek is a foaming torrent, interrupted here and there by cascades and rapids. Though when its bed is full it may be called a river, I should not advise a steamboat captain, however bold and skilful, to attempt to navigate it with a cargo of even the toughest goods. But its banks are often picturesque and diversified so as to lend an enchantment to the landscape. Some of the wealthiest citizens of Troy had for this reason thought of building their residences in the neighborhood, and thus the celebrated Pawling Avenue had been laid out on the map of the city, though the ground was, in fact, without the limits of the city. At the east end of the projected avenue there happens to be a small village, or rather hamlet, whose vicinity is the picture of loveliness and rural bliss, chiefly on account of the diminutive Poestenkill, which is there as placid as a lake and in many places runs along under a perfect bower of willow-trees. As I had already several times visited this locality to carry the blessings of religion to some sick Christian of my parish, I said to myself that if my birds had established their temporary quarters in that neighborhood the rogues had fallen upon a paradise, for at a very short distance from the avenue and the village the country almost deserves that name. The village is called Albia.

I set out, therefore, very early, taking with me the materials of a lunch, as I wished to enjoy the pleasure of a solitary picnic at least, in case this ramble should not be more successful than had been the first. It was at the end of August and the weather was lovely; an abundant rain a few days previously had cooled the atmosphere and refreshed the trees and the underbrush, renewing their green lustre as if it had been only the end of June.

Along Pawling Avenue I saw very few sparrows. There are in that direction too many houses, and the birds had deserted the neighborhood almost as completely as our own in South Troy.

But as soon as I had passed the village of Albia I was again in the midst of sparrowdom, and the further I advanced into the interior of this unfrequented territory the more the sparrow population seemed to increase. None, however, of those I was looking for had yet fallen under my eyes.

I made up my mind to eat my lunch as soon as I should find a perfectly secluded spot where no urchin could see me and no harvester could guess my object. For there were here and there harvesters in the fields and boys along the creek, and the common opinion is that no one eats in the fields but a—*tramp*.

At last I espied a shadowy lane of willow-trees, as regular as if it had been planted by the hand of man. These trees skirted a most lovely bank of the miniature river; and, exactly as if my personal comfort had been studied in detail by an attentive purveyor, a clean rock covered with moss and lichen offered me a seat so conveniently placed that I could with one hand feed the minnows in the stream and with the other throw the remaining crumbs to the sparrows under the willow-trees.

I do not like to eat alone; but if I cannot have a human being with me at table I like to have on one side a small *aquarium* with goldfish and on the other a cage or two of canary birds. That simple pleasure God had offered me in that solitude where I was going to take my lunch. I began in earnest, for I was hungry; but I did not forget to scatter in profusion the gifts of Ceres, as a pagan would have said—the phenomenal elements of wheat, which often become the veil of a hidden Saviour, as a Christian prefers to express it.

The meal was already more than half finished; troops of minnows were actively munching at the bread spread on the water, and as large a number of sparrows were hurriedly coming down from the willow-trees in the near neighborhood of the rock where I was seated, when, lo and behold! old General Twit-Twat himself rushed through the crowd and alighted just at my feet. I was indeed a happy man! But the good fellow was not alone of his tribe. All his progeny followed in his wake, of course after his Amazon, and the numerous army extended as far as the end of the lane formed by the willow-trees.

Strange to say, I soon found out that the native rascals had chosen the same camping-ground. It was impossible to conjecture if there had been fights among the two parties during this time of summering. But it was evident that the former estrangement between them around the poplar-trees in South Troy was continued here on the banks of the Poestenkill at the farther end of Pawling Avenue. The natives did not come near me, probably, I first thought, on account of the large number of Twit-Twats by which I was surrounded. The question, however, which I came to investigate was now clear to my mind. The sparrows *would* go back to South Troy; they were residing temporarily only in their new district, where they had no nests and no holes for the winter, and scarcely any means of constructing new ones. But before returning home I determined to study, during a part of the afternoon, their way of living when out of their usual haunts during August and September. These precious observations can be compressed in a few pregnant paragraphs.

That it was a real rustication, on the exact model of the one indulged during the same months by our fashionable gentlemen and ladies, can be proved by all the chief details of both.

First, it is for both a season of bathing and drinking waters—with the remark, however, that it is done by the sparrows in a more natural, primitive, and sensible manner. As soon as they had finished their simple meal around me they all flew to the banks of the lovely Poestenkill. Wherever there was a little pool of clear, lucid water at the edge of the stream they jumped into it, two, three, or four together, and there was such a splashing, such an innocent tussle among them as it was a pleasure to see. It was easy to understand that the great object was ablution—that is, to clean themselves thoroughly, and to clear away from their wings, tails, and feathers generally all dust and unseemly taint which might mar their natural beauty. But together with that they wished to amuse themselves; and with what a grace they did it! How clumsy in comparison is the ducking of two rustic swains who also pretend to develop their muscular strength and give a show of their agility in swimming! Go and look at the sparrows when they bathe, and say which you prefer.

And bathing was not then their only occupation, for they drank too. Have you ever remarked with what stateliness, demureness little birds drink? Their body does not move, but their little head goes up and down with almost the regularity of clockwork; and their little necks—how they are stretched! how gracefully they bend first and assume a perpendicular position afterwards! and their bright eyes seem to show that they relish that innocent degustation. After having observed it a thousand times

I have no doubt that they find in the different kinds of waters as many tastes as the most fastidious wine-bibber thinks he discovers in his claret or Delaware.

Think you, gentle reader, that fashionable people who go to Saratoga in order to drink the waters find as pleasurable a sensation in swallowing their three glasses of *Congress* as my little pets experienced along the banks of the Poestenkill? For my own part I cannot believe it.

Secondly, both human beings and birds enjoy their dances—or their *hops*, as they say at Saratoga—during rustication-time. Let us examine for a moment the lively dances of the sparrows. They have first the *duet*, in which they are but two, and in which they use their feet only. Everybody has seen this, but few indeed have paid attention to it. Two sparrows, flying rapidly from two distant parts of the common field, perch on two neighboring twigs of the same tree. At once the duet begins. It consists merely in changing places; but the operation is often very rapid and must be extremely healthy and reinvigorating. It is so natural in them that, when they are infamously reduced to slavery by unfeeling man and are incarcerated two in a single cage, they set at it sometimes for a good part of the forenoon. There is still a worse situation for the poor birds, and this is the total isolation to which they are condemned when unjust and cruel man sentences one of them to solitary confinement. The lonely prisoner continues to hop as if he had a companion. I can assure my reader that in absolute freedom, particularly during rustication, they frequently enjoy the duet among themselves; and I saw a great many pairs dancing in this manner in the willow-trees along the Poestenkill Creek.

As it would be tedious to describe all their motions when these are regulated by the terpsichorean art (in which they succeed much better than men do at Long Branch), we shall select as an instance *the grand aerial dance*, for which several trees at least are required in close contiguity. The sparrows join in it by a dozen at a time, and they use their wings rather than their feet for it, so that men cannot possibly rival them in this dance. It succeeds admirably when, as I have often seen from my windows in South Troy, they have poplar-trees at their disposal. These graceful plants, as everybody knows, are tall, slender, and regular in form from bottom to top. If planted in a row, with an interval of eight or ten inches between the foliage of each, they are well suited for this frolicsome exercise. The birds begin at one end of the row of trees, following each other closely. They issue forth in great glee from behind the first tree, twittering and dancing as they go; then flying rapidly, and passing between the second and third poplars, they disappear for a moment behind the foliage, and come out again in the same order between the two next trees. Thus they go on until the last tree is reached, when they begin again in an inverse order. The great object of each seems to be to overreach the bird that precedes, and take its place in the dance. I have no doubt that if the bird that comes out the last at parting could be the first to arrive at the last poplar, he would acquire great renown among his country-people, and—who knows?—in one of their secret meetings he might receive a crown of blossoms of *forget-me-nots*, as the winner at the races of Olympia in Greece received a crown of laurel.

Thirdly and lastly, the gentlemen and ladies who spend a month or two in summer at any of our spas—Saratoga, or Long Branch, or Cape May—intend to rest from their labors and recruit for the next ten months of commercial or industrial speculation. This rest they find not merely in drinking and bathing and dancing, but principally, perhaps, in reading sensational novels, of which they usually have a large valise full. In this, I acknowledge, men have an advantage over sparrows. I am not, however, without hope that with the rapid headway that *progress* is going on in this century the time shall come when man will not be the only being in animated nature having the ability to read. In that case it cannot be doubted that birds, and sparrows in particular, which are among the most intelligent of vertebrals (see Webster), will share in all the advantages of the reading gift. Mr. Darwin's ingenious theories give us the hope that this happy consummation of the evolutionary process will not be too long delayed. A very forcible writer in the *North American Review* for 1873 remarks, with a profound acumen, that "there is more difficulty for a Simoid ape, armed only with a stone, to progress so far as to make a hatchet of the stone than for the same interesting animal, armed now with its hatchet, to invent the whole of chemistry, not to speak of mental philosophy." But the same Simoid ape has already progressed so far as to make a hatchet of a stone; therefore, etc.

To apply this remarkable syllogism to the case of the Twit-Twats and natives, we may say, likewise, that it was more difficult for sparrows, living at first without head-covering under the canopy of heaven, to *invent* the comfortable habit of sleeping in a cottage than it is for the same birds, now on the open road to civilization, to *create* for themselves all the arts of man, including his literature.

After this long disquisition the reader will readily acknowledge that there is every year a time of rustication for sparrows, and I can now proceed with my narrative.

My business being accomplished with every possible feeling of satisfaction, I prepared to return home. I could no longer be afraid of meeting with harvesters or urchins, for I had disposed of all the materials for my lunch; and even in case I should think proper to stop on my way and stretch myself on the grass under a tree, there would be no possibility of mistaking me for a wretched *tramp* hurriedly partaking of a stolen dinner. All fear as to my respectability was consequently banished from my mind, and, after having concluded my ornithological exploration, I walked along leisurely.

Soon I perceived a crowd of boys coming directly towards me, and I had no motive for endeavoring to avoid them. I counted as many as ten of them, and they appeared to be discussing among themselves a very serious affair. As soon as they came within a hailing distance, "Well, my dear boys," said I to them, "what is the matter? I hope no great accident has happened you." "No accident to any of us," replied one of them, "but a sad one for a small bird that we have just found under a tree, and we cannot agree among ourselves how its carcass came there."

These few words interested me, as there was question of a bird, although a dead one. I asked: "Can you show me its carcass? I may find out the cause of its death."

"Here it is," said the same boy, who had it all the time in his hand, and to my great surprise he gave me a real defunct sparrow. Looking at it more attentively, I became convinced that it was the dear old native patriarch that had so often delighted my eyes when he occupied the bird-cottage under my window, and whom I had not seen in that day's ramble. It is true, the body was completely emaciated; death had made a great change in him; but the form of his bill, the color of his feathers, the whole of his phiz, in fact, told me it was *he!*

"Well," said I to the boys, "what do you think was the cause of *his* death?" I considered a bird of that species almost as a reasonable being.

"We cannot agree about it," replied the boy. "It could not be a shot from a fowler's gun, as there is no hole in the whole carcass. It was not wounded nor mangled by its *friends*, the other sparrows, as there is no scar or hole in its body. It might have been killed by the wind and rain, or it might have starved to death. We disagree about that."

"Well, my friends," said I, "you are wide of the mark in all your conjectures. I knew the bird, and he must have died either of *apoplexy* or of *gastritis*; besides all this, he had pretty well run through the whole span of his life, since he must have enjoyed at least a decade of years—"

Here I remarked that I was using a language which might be as hard as Hebrew for the poor boys.

"All I can say," I added in conclusion, "is that he must have died a natural death. Let me have him." And instead of the sparrow I handed their spokesman a bright quarter of a dollar. There was enough to furnish plenty of candy for the whole troop, and they all departed with joy.

Left alone with the body of my old friend, I began to muse over what must have happened, and also over the future consequences of so sad a catastrophe. The more I looked at him the more I was convinced that I was right in the conjectures I had expressed to the boys. The emaciation of the poor old patriarch might have been caused by a protracted disease of the stomach, and *gastritis* would have been the natural result; or old age might have caused the induration of the vascular system around the heart, and then the blood, instead of coursing through his veins, would have rushed to the *cerebrum* and produced *apoplexy*. I was right as to science, but wrong in the circumstances in which I displayed my knowledge. The boys could not understand a word of it.

But what affected me most painfully was the foresight of what would henceforward happen. Old Mr. Native was the only one who could keep his contumacious progeny in a somewhat peaceful state of mind. He alone could prevent them from breaking constantly out into open war. It was even with great difficulty that he kept

Final Victory of the Twit-Twats.

them within certain bounds. What would happen when both Twit-Twats and natives should return to their former quarters? The gentle mate of the patriarch would be altogether unable to grapple with the difficulty after the death of her spouse.

It was very likely that the standing aloof of the whole native camp which I had remarked that very day in the peaceful region of the Upper Poestenkill came more from the recent death of their chief than from any former feeling of antipathy for the Twit-Twats. They already felt that they were left to their own uncertain guidance, and they may have been even then arranging their plans of conflict and open war, perhaps under the new young leader.

These were the sorrowful thoughts which accompanied me as far as South Troy, and I need not assure the reader that, once arrived, I gave a decent burial to my friend at the foot of his own poplar-tree, and waited anxiously for the next month, which was to bring back the wanderers. They arrived at the end of September. They evidently followed the course of the Lower Poestenkill and of the Hollow Road, which below the Falls are quite near to each other.

Soon all the trees around the church and the rectory swarmed with them; they rested again on my window-sills; their shrill twitterings and their frisky gambols gave life again to the whole neighborhood, and I opened my eyes wide to see if they would reoccupy their former dwellings without contention; for, as the reader knows, I expected a fierce war.

Fortunately, those who came first were all Twit-Twats. The old general was the first to appear, and it was proper on such an auspicious occasion that he should be at their head. He immediately occupied his ancient quarters in the bird-cottage. To complete my happiness, his mate was with him, and both seemed to have fairly recruited during their absence, though they were undoubtedly getting old. The native side of the little bird-house remained empty for a short time, but with the rear-guard of the Twit-Twat troops the old female native patriarch came at last and took possession of her desolate quarters. We all know why she came alone, and that at this moment her dead mate was already mouldering in his grave at the foot of the same tree.

In my conversation with the boys who had found his corpse I briefly gave my conjectures on the true causes of his demise; but as this little volume is intended to convey all possible information on the natural history of sparrows, it is proper to say a word in general as to the way that their mortal course usually comes to an end.

Naturalists experienced a great deal of trouble before they could find out how birds die, when their demise is not the result of violence. They pretend, it is true, that the greatest number of them meet their death in this last sudden manner. I am convinced that this is a mistake, at least in the case of the sparrows. Few perish under the claws of the hawk; more are caught by, and become the victims of, the cruelty of boys; some expire of want or are killed outright by the pitiless storm; but with all this their multiplication is so rapid and their natural life so short that the immense majority of them must run through the full career allotted them by Providence, and literally die of old age, since very few animals in the state of nature end their life through sickness. But the difficulty is to ascertain the various circumstances which accompany and follow their last day. Necropolises of birds have never been found except in Egypt, and in that ancient country their corpses were embalmed by foolish pagans who literally worshipped them; they were not solemnly and piously interred by their kindred or friends. It is generally supposed, and in the main it must be true, that when they feel their end approaching they retire to some hole in the ground, or in an old wall, or in some rock difficult of access, and there gradually die away in solitude, without much suffering, it is true, but without any alleviating circumstance, as happens in the case of man, who usually expires surrounded by his friends, with all the help that charity and religion can afford.

CHAPTER XI.

WAR AGAIN AND CONFUSION—FINAL SUCCESS OF THE TWIT-TWATS.

THE native crew did not reappear in South Troy until all the Twit-Twats had returned. They came in sufficiently good order, not too hastily, and again took possession of all the places they had occupied previous to their rustication. This was fortunate, for no one could say what would have taken place had the two hostile nations arrived together. Such as it was, at the final coming of the natives it was evident that a revolution was imminent, as modern historians have often to say of human beings in our age. The absence of the venerable male native bird, whose aspect alone used previously to keep his numerous broods in order, could not but produce within a short time a general change in the obstinate and ill-regulated native republic. The gentle mate of the old defunct bird, reduced to solitude in her part of the cottage, had no inclination, had she the power even, to assume the reins of government. Her neighbors, the old Twit-Twats, were in possession of their apartment; but how long would they continue quiet in their quarters was something that remained to be seen.

Soon, indeed, the hostile intentions of the rascally colony were unmistakably manifested; and the insolent crew was kept united by the unanimous desire of injuring those whom they called aliens and enemies. This was the first stage of the war, which must be briefly described. The native birds, although deprived of their former chieftain, and not seeming to feel inclined to elect another to place at their head—for instance, the bold fellow with the ugly scar, of whom a word was said before—had, nevertheless, at first a common aim which preserved them from gaunt anarchy. The hatred of the Twit-Twats was their only guide; but it was a fierce guide, which gave to each of them an enormous individual strength, and to their whole body very great power. Their main object evidently was to drive away their enemies, occupy their places, and afterwards destroy them if they could.

They proceeded systematically in this intention; and though still without a commander, their instinctive fury took the place of one. First they meant to take possession of the whole bird-cottage by *evicting* the noble Twit-Twat couple from it, as well as the forlorn female native. Whenever a single one of the three poor old birds appeared unaccompanied by any of their progeny or friends, it was immediately and eagerly followed by two or three ferocious enemies, who evidently found a keen delight in mocking, cruelly pecking, and pursuing without mercy. Hence even the repairing of the nests inside of the cottage was neglected; there was scarcely time to collect food enough for sustenance.

The constancy of these attacks proved to me that it was a system on the part of the young natives; and it was done in such a manner, at such a distance from me, that I could not possibly help my dear little pets, and was reduced closely to examine all the vicissitudes of this barbarous war.

After a great number of these individual contests the cunning crew grew bold enough to lay siege to the cottage itself—not, it is true, in a regular way, "by passages and advanced works which cover the besiegers from the enemy's fire," as they say in books on military engineering. The sparrows have not yet progressed far enough in civilization to reach that degree of military science. The Twit-Twats, besides, being settled all around, would probably not have allowed them to stand in arms for weeks and months together before this beloved fortress. The turbulent and scoundrelly pack evidently intended to carry it by stratagem, or rather by an assault. Five or six at a time, they often, as if peacefully inclined, alighted on the little platform of the bird-cottage, but always on the Twit-Twat side. They appeared to respect, for the time being, the last refuge of poor Mrs. Native, who had, however, no influence whatever over them. Their *respect* for her merely consisted in not noticing her movements, and leaving her temporarily unmolested in her side of the cottage. But they appeared very inquisitive as to the Twit-Twat quarters. They peeped into them, and looked impudently inside of the room, where the two old stagers, keeping quiet, were perhaps cowering in a corner with fear and trembling. This, nevertheless, was a mere conjecture of mine, as I could not have any ocular demonstration of what happened in the interior.

On one occasion old General Twit-Twat took a noble revenge on the inquisitive fellows. Seeing them, from his recess, pressed, or rather jammed, up against the outside projection, he suddenly rushed out and brushed them all off with his wings, beak, and claws; and, having cleared the platform of their hateful presence, he evidently dared them to combat by his shrill twittering, his turning right and left with indignation and scorn, and chiefly by the tossing of his head, on which stood erect the large and rough red and black plumes that served the place of the waving horse-hair, the adornment of Achilles' helmet.

The native crew, discomfited for this once, watched for the moment when he should be out and only his Amazon remain inside. The moment came, and one of them dared not only to peep and look in, but even to enter. He came out, however, more quickly than he had gone in, and it is said that several of his feathers remained in the beak of the courageous female, who, as we all know, was not exactly a novice in the noble art of self-defence.

These attacks, however, became at last so frequent, fierce, and positively annoying that the old couple, always fond of peace in spite of the names they bore, had to think of moving to more quiet quarters. They suddenly left empty their room in the cottage, which was immediately seized upon by their ferocious neighbors and emptied of all its contents in the shape of dry grass, hay, straw, paper, and nondescript odds and ends of every possible nature.

Shortly after this the young native bird who had appeared the previous season so obsequious to his old sire (and who now evidently aspired to be the new leader of his tribe, though so far without success) grew colder and colder every day and more and more insolent to the forlorn female left alone in the cottage, though she was, as all knew, his fond parent. After various distressing scenes of insult and contumely the poor old bird also left her dwelling, and was ever after constantly seen in Twit-Twat company. She had been turned out of the society of her natural friends, and was duly adopted by those who originally were thought to be her enemies.

The first object of the open war undertaken by the natives was now accomplished. They had the Twit-Twat fortress in their power, and could proceed to execute bolder and vaster designs. Their next purpose was, in fact, nothing less than to drive away from their neighborhood the whole race of sparrows opposed to them, and to destroy, as far as might be, the former prosperous Twit-Twat empire.

This horrible project kept them more united than ever; and as their troops were very numerous, since the previous summer's increase had made them a large army, they had a fair prospect of victory. The hostile camp, nevertheless, was also very large for the same reason—the statistics to prove it have been exact and conclusive; and the Twit-Twats having a leader accomplished in every respect, the odds certainly were in their favor. I could never ascertain why the other party obstinately refused to acknowledge the claims of the young would-be leader.

It would be extremely interesting to follow all the evolutions and manœuvres which soon began; but as the first result of several heavy battles was unfavorable to the party of right, I beg to be excused from giving the detailed narrative. It would be too distressing to my feelings; and the reader must be content to know that by the end of October the Twit-Twat ranks were dispersed—they had withdrawn far beyond their former limits, and their empire of the previous year seemed to have melted into air.

Their enemies were now masters of the entire field; no one appeared to oppose them, and they could boast of having succeeded in all their plans. Yet this was the great cause of their final overthrow.

No longer having foreign competitors, being left besides to their own guidance and totally deprived of a chieftain, they had no unity of plan, for the hatred of the Twit-Twats, which had first united them, had disappeared with its object. They were totally abandoned to the fury of their growing passions, and their camp soon became a very bedlam of obstinacy and bad manners. They forgot the great principle which, as was seen, is the solid foundation of peace among sparrows—namely, the sacredness of property vested in those who have obtained possession of a home. Nowhere else have I ever seen birds molested by other sparrows in the quarters where they had fairly established themselves. But I could be surprised at no excess of that kind after their shameful conduct in and around the celebrated bird-cottage. We have just seen how they unjustly got possession of it, and it was the first breach of the fundamental rule among them. After this everything might be expected.

Having once combined for such a purpose against the hated Twit-Twats, they each felt an irrepressible desire of satisfying their avidity by forcibly occupying the hole or the nest which might be the most convenient, even when this was in the lawful possession of a brother native. Thus was the seed of a frightful anarchy scattered broadcast through their extensive commonwealth. And as I never felt a strong inclination in favor of that brood, it was, I confess, without deep regret that I became the attentive witness of the numerous events which accompanied among them the usual process by which cities and republics are destroyed among men.

It soon became an interesting study for me. For instance, in this very month of October a nest that had been built with more than usual care in the third poplar to the left of my window was eagerly occupied by an active native pair as soon as the Twit-Twats withdrew. After a full week of occupancy they could claim to be the lawful owners of it, according to sparrow jurisprudence. Still another pair, left as yet without a home, arrived, under my eyes, with the evident intention of *evicting* the occupants and forcibly seizing upon what did not belong to them. The contest was sharp, bloody, and decisive. I shall not describe the incidents of it, but, after a fight lasting half a day, the peaceful occupants were thrown out, and the unjust invaders ensconced themselves for the following night, without any apparent compunction or remorse, in a bed which they had not labored to make. *Sic vos non vobis, etc.*

A much more distressing case of rapine was also witnessed by me. A native couple had evidently returned from rustication without being in the least recruited in health —nay, with all the signs of debility and helplessness. Having at an opportune moment taken possession of a fine empty hole under the eaves of a small outside building which could be seen from one of the windows of the rectory, they thought themselves secure—the more so that their bad health would have been sufficient to excite the pity of the benevolent. But a pugnacious pair of cowards, who would not have dared attack a couple of birds in sound condition, did not blush to peck at them and drive them off, probably to die under the canopy of heaven.

I could quote hundreds of such cases, but I forbear and leave something to the reader's imagination Yet it is important to mention other causes of strife, for the sinful longing after other people's property was far from being the only one. I am convinced that among many of them there were deep feelings of animosity produced by months, and perhaps years, of personal contentions. I remarked particularly two of them who were evidently brooding over long memories of past wrongs. They often looked askance at one another, and seemed acted upon by deep reciprocal suspicions. The more remarkable of these two scamps was the very first-born of the old native patriarchs, whose scar has been already mentioned more than once, and who had for a long time aspired to be the leader of the tribe. The other was a far inferior bird in point of blood, but as bold and unprincipled as the first. From mere suspicion and mistrust they gradually gave each other strong proofs of mutual hatred, and, what was far worse, they influenced many birds who were already too much disposed to vent their anger on everybody and everything, so that I soon witnessed many scenes of riot and violence. Perhaps the unrecognized claims of Mr. Native, Jr., were at the bottom of the strife.

The fierce contest between these two savage enemies became at last irrepressible, and it was soon followed by a universal commotion within the whole turbulent tribe. This *commotion* was very different from the conflict of the previous summer between natives and Twit-Twats. It was not a pitched battle of clan against clan, of the virtuous against the depraved; it was an internecine contest of rascally birds bent on nothing but mutual extermination. You could not see—as previously described—two well-defined armies, one fighting for right, the other for might. Might alone was now the universal aim among them; and, as its object was different for each, nothing could be seen of that unity which had been the fatal cause of the success recorded at the beginning of this month of October. Hence, although they certainly formed groups of combatants, and seemed to have war-cries of their own which rallied a small number of aspirants to fame and honor, yet, on the whole, it was a medley, and it looked as if sparrow society was decomposed almost in its primitive elements.

One remarkable day they gave me the awful spectacle of absolute anarchy, for they were all desperately contending, in complete disorder, with beaks, claws, wings—every weapon, in fact, that nature had given them. The dead and dying covered the ground; and, frightful to relate, those who had not yet given up the ghost, but were in the throes of agony, still fought as desperately as if they were not all engulfed in the same misery, and could still improve their individual condition by the total destruction of the others.

It was after a struggle of this kind, lasting the better part of a whole afternoon, that the two young desperadoes with the mention of whom this description began, being stripped of most of their feathers in the general engagement, fell furiously upon one another, uttering screams which might be taken for articulate threats of revenge and expressions of the deepest hatred. They fought one another to death, which they both met with all the horrible circumstances of an irrepressible and loathsome fury.

This state of *gaunt anarchy*, as it has been called, had lasted several days when the Twit-Twats, who, since they had been driven off from the field, had completely disappeared, began to show themselves in twos and threes, all exhibiting signs of the greatest curiosity and interest. I knew not exactly whence they were coming back, having had no time to follow them into the interior of the country; though I hardly believe that in their flight they had retreated as far as their summer paradise on the banks of the Upper Poestenkill. They were likely ensconced in the shady ravines of what is called in Troy the *Hollow Road*, through which they had formerly returned

Return from Rustication along the Poestenkill and the Hollow Road.

from rustication. In their temporary retreat they had not fared very badly; they were apparently as jolly and sprightly as ever—in fact, sleek and in good condition. The first I saw surprised me by their agility and visible strength. I concluded that if the whole tribe had enjoyed as excellent quarters as these good fellows they could shortly show fight, and there might be fun before long.

The first Twit-Twats, however, that arrived on their former grounds evidently did not carry their pretensions so far as immediately to engage in the fray and help their enemies to destroy each other. I soon perceived that they were merely scouts sent by the old general to reconnoitre, and that they must have received very strict orders not to display their fighting propensity. A few of them who were bold enough to rest on the sill of one of my windows clearly showed what they were about; they seemed to look very inquisitively only into the affairs of their sworn opponents, in order faithfully to report the true state of affairs. They looked as sharp as "detectives," but nothing more. Let the reader be persuaded that I was not rash in my conjectures. After frequent and protracted observations of these birds' habits I am fully convinced that in front of their "armies" there are always "scouts," and that when you see the keen explorers the solid troops are not far behind.

In confirmation of this truth it is a positive fact that very shortly after the "scouts" had appeared the main "army" came; and it was a glorious sight to enjoy, chiefly as my dear friend himself, the original patriarch, fresh and active still under his eleven summers, occupied his proud position at the head of a well-organized soldiery. The first view brought me the conviction that complete success was near and infallible. The natives, on account of their absolute disorganization, could not offer any resistance. They had no leader; and, besides, at that moment they thought only of fighting among themselves. They had, moreover, lost a great part of their forces; and their own dead strewed the ground, not only under the poplar-trees and all around the rectory and the church, but even in so sacred a spot as the sisters' convent and the holy garden where the good nuns usually walked.

It was at once a complete sweep which did not require the whole of that afternoon. I do not know how many native birds remained after the fight, but I can personally aver that my eyes never saw a single one of them after that day.

The greatest trouble the Twit-Twats found was to shelter themselves in their former abodes during the short time of the afternoon which remained from the moment of victory till sunset. It is well known that these birds retire into their holes and nests as soon as the orb of the sun sinks under the distant horizon. They had consequently scarcely half an hour to make their choice and occupy in peace their individual quarters. But such was the order established among them by their experienced commander that I could not perceive any quarrelling among them in so delicate an operation; and when night arrived not only was the old Twit-Twat empire restored without the loss of a single one of the tribe, but peace reigned supreme and could not be disturbed any more.

CHAPTER XII.

CHRISTMAS AGAIN—THE WINTER FESTIVAL OF THE SPARROWS.

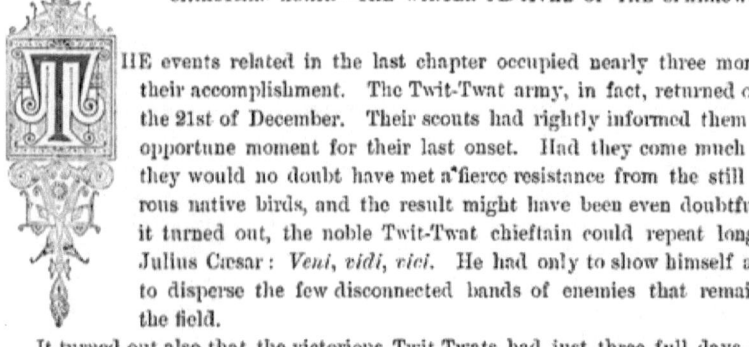

HE events related in the last chapter occupied nearly three months in their accomplishment. The Twit-Twat army, in fact, returned only on the 21st of December. Their scouts had rightly informed them of the opportune moment for their last onset. Had they come much sooner they would no doubt have met a fierce resistance from the still numerous native birds, and the result might have been even doubtful. As it turned out, the noble Twit-Twat chieftain could repeat long after Julius Cæsar: *Veni, vidi, vici*. He had only to show himself at once to disperse the few disconnected bands of enemies that remained in the field.

It turned out also that the victorious Twit-Twats had just three full days to rest before the arrival of Christmas. Had they delayed until the very eve of that great festival they would not have been able to enjoy it fully, but would have been obliged to spend the whole of it mournfully in a much-needed rest, either in their holes or in the immediate vicinity. And they would have had to postpone the celebration of their own *winter festival*, which generally happens to fall on that day, until New Year's, or perhaps until the 6th of January. Had they been French birds they might not have felt the change so much, for the French generally consider New Year's, or *la fête des Rois*, as being on a par with the 25th of December. But the Twit-Twats, being Irish to the backbone, could not adopt such new-fangled notions; they strictly stuck to the old Catholic calendar, which has always placed the birth of the Saviour far above the day of the Circumcision or the Epiphany. It was, therefore, much better that they should come just when they did.

And first of all for three full days they enjoyed the delightful feeling of peace which had finally been granted them with every prospect of a long duration. Peace, heavenly Peace! How is it that thou art not better appreciated by men or sparrows? How many blessings thou bringest in thy train which alone can make life enjoyable and this world an anticipation of heaven! Domestic contentment, national felicity, social happiness can be truly relished only in the total absence of contention and war. Wherever there is strife life, in the palace or the cottage alike, is cheerless and gloomy. The highest success in war infallibly brings evils without number, which the nations soon feel keenly. As to the social ties which make men inwardly happy by the vivid consciousness that there is a true brotherhood in mankind, it is during a profound peace alone that their strength is felt and their influence paramount.

These things have been repeated thousands of times since the beginning of the world; still men and birds continue to engage in contention upon the flimsiest pretexts, such as a few disputed rods of territory, an acre or so of marshy ground, some bare rock or other at the end of a long chain of mountains, or any *in*appreciable advantage of that kind.

At least at this moment peace seems to be deeply felt not only by the gleeful Twit-Twats, but by the numerous population of human beings residing in Troy and its vicinity. They know that the Prince of Peace is born anew, and their hearts are overflowing with "the milk of human kindness." It is Christmas morning, and joy is felt in the still and slightly frosty air. Towards the east you may already see the first blush of dawn; but it is still night overhead, and myriads of stars are twinkling in the blue firmament. Hear the silvery bells already sending their peals of jubilee through the tranquil atmosphere. Come out, all ye sincere Christians, come out of your peaceful homes; like the shepherds, you are called around a Saviour's cradle. Clad in your best attire, travel in groups along the dimly-lighted streets. There is the church yonder, and streams of light begin to pour through its windows. There is time yet to reach it leisurely, and the bells continue to peal with both solemnity and merriment. Still, hasten on, hasten on; it is far better to be inside when the first notes of the organ shall be heard, soft as a whisper and tender as a love-ditty, than to linger outside on slippery sidewalks or the hard bed of the road.

Who has not in his life experienced all the pleasant sensations of such an hour? Early Christmas morning is a happy moment which comes only once in the year, and is invariably treasured up afterwards in the sweetest corner of the memory. The age of the person makes scarcely any difference in the quality of the impression. A little girl of seven can almost as well appreciate the Babe of Bethlehem as her grandmother. She knows that His name is Jesus, which means Saviour. She has learned that His birth was announced by angels and ascertained by shepherds; that kings came afterwards before His crib, and thus high and low, rich and poor, acknowledged Him as their Redeemer and their God. And, finally, she knows something of His laborious life and cruel death on a cross, of which she is reminded every time her lips are pressed upon the crucifix.

What more need be known by the full-grown man or by the fully-developed woman? Have we not all of us the same main idea of the infant Saviour, and something of the same love for Him when our heart is not taken up by some unworthy passion? Christmas morning, therefore, bears absolutely the same aspect for all Christians of any age, sex, or condition.

See them at this moment filling the streets of Troy and the roads in the neighborhood. For it is not only around the celebrated poplar-trees, and in and about the con-

St. Joseph's Church on early Christmas Morning.

vent, and throughout the whole extent of the renowned *mayordom**—to coin a necessary word—of South Troy that the Christmas festival brings joy to the heart of man, woman, or child; but as far up north as the last limits of Lansingburg; as far down south as Greenbush itself, called sometimes East Albany; as far east as the distant source of the Poestenkill; and west as far as old Schenectady itself, which boasts of an existence older than that of Albany, or Fort Orange—consequently, in a good slice of Rensselaer County, and in a not inconsiderable portion of that of Albany—the scene we have to consider is enacted on gigantic proportions. Every one knows that the same thing takes place everywhere on earth. But the scope of our story limits us to that part of the world whose centre is the city which is now blessed by the joyful presence of our dear Twit-Twats. It includes, therefore, besides a prosperous metropolis—Troy deserves the name—several large towns, such as Lansingburg, Cohoes, and West Troy, and an indefinite number of smaller villages disseminated at random over the whole territory.

In all these places thousands upon thousands of happy people are thinking of one thing only—that is, Christmas morning; and this thing implies the two sweetest figures that the earth has ever seen, Jesus and His Mother Mary! Look at the number of churches which are at this moment blazing with light and resonant with music. Skilful and ready hands have spent more than a week in cleaning and adorning them; the forest has furnished its evergreens and the hothouse its garlands of sweet-scented flowers. It is the reign of peace and harmony and tender feelings, and the churches are the necessary centres of all those sweet emotions. We might limit ourselves to consider solely those churches where the Divine Babe can be found not only represented outside of the altar reclining on a crib, but actually present in the tabernacle to rejoice His faithful adorers, repose a moment on their lips, and go to rest in their enraptured hearts. Many such places, thank God! can be found in the happy district that has been just described; and on that day they seem to have lost their individual names of St. Patrick's and St. Bridget's and St. Peter's, even those of St. Mary's and St. Joseph's, to fill the worshipper's memory by the only recollection of the Cave of Bethlehem. We might do so, and not even think of other places of worship, without any one casting on us a slur on account of our exclusiveness; because our Church alone goes as far back as the true day of the Saviour's birth and the true spot where Mary received Him in her arms.

But we must remember that all those who celebrate the day with respect and some-

---

* Twenty-seven years ago I became acquainted with a certain Mr. Martin Russell, who lived in a cottage at the southwest corner of Third and Madison Streets, in Troy. He related to me that more than thirty years before he lived alone on the same spot, which was then a wilderness. Soon, however, two new-comers arrived, and one winter evening the three together, standing around the stove, agreed to call the place South Troy, and the new friends of Mr. Russell elected him mayor of the village *in perpetuum*—that is, during his life. Thenceforth he took the title of his dignity, and in my time it would have been almost an insult not to address him as Mr. Mayor. Poor Martin Russell! He was a genial man and friendly to everybody. He has, nevertheless, ceased to be mayor of South Troy, as his dignity was conferred only for life, and he is, I think, now dead.

thing like unto veneration, all those who recognize in the Child just born their God and Redeemer, have at least a faint recollection of the profound mysteries which have always made of the 25th of December one of the greatest, if not absolutely the happiest, day of the whole Christian year. Whoever recognizes God as his Creator, and the only-begotten Son of God as his Saviour, has a right to the beautiful name of Christian; and, consequently, for that day which is the only one we can now think of we will consider as our brethren those numerous flocks of happy people also who go to the Episcopalian churches of St. Paul and of St. John and of the Holy Cross, and wheresoever are inscribed in evergreen the well-known words of Isaias: " A Child is born to us, and a Son is given to us, . . . and His name shall be called Wonderful, Counsellor, God the Mighty, the Father of the world to come, the Prince of peace"; for they also have listened to the inward voice which calls them to adore with humility "the Word made flesh," the Son of the Father in eternity and of the meek Mary in time. Unfortunately all these people will not find the tabernacle with its precious gift, as everything with them is representative and not substantial; they will enjoy a shadow only, as the Jews did of old, but this shadow is at least a sweet one, and who knows if God will not one day tear asunder the veil and show them the substance? At least they do not share in the infatuation of those dark Puritans who made Christmas a day of gloom, and would not on that day allow their choir, if they had such a thing, to intone a hymn in honor of the infant God, of whom their Bible spoke to their eyes but not to their heart.

But, thank God again! these children of Knox and Calvin have been at last humanized by the universal joy which Christmas day inspires in the hearts of the hardest. What a miracle, such as the hand of the Almighty alone could perform: the descendants of the harsh soldiers of Cromwell in England, and of the stern Huguenots in France, no longer object to a celebration of some kind in their churches or to hear the organ peal, and they even sing something like our own *Venite adoremus!*

It is a step, though a reluctant one, in the right direction. But will they come so far towards us as to exhibit in their meeting-houses on that day the image of Mary with the Child on her knees, with old Joseph behind, and with the ox and ass on both sides of the crib? If they do, I, for one, answer for their salvation.

But to return to our theme. Was not all this a proof that there was joy in Troy on that special day of Christmas, 187-? How different from that of the year previous! The reader remembers that the 25th of December which ushered in the unfortunate Twit-Twats on the broad stage of our story was one of gloom and almost of despair. To appreciate the complete contrast between the two epochs, think not only of the disconsolate and woe-begone condition of the birds a year ago, so sprightly and hopeful to-day. Remember, too, what was then said of many men for whom Christmas brings no change in their wretched condition, and who have to spend it in their miserable cabins with nothing on their table different from their ordinary meagre fare. This had been the case the year before in many houses in Troy, owing to a long suspension of work; but on this happy Christmas of 187- there did not seem to be a single dwelling-house in the city or in the country round about without an appetizing dinner temptingly smoking on a well-prepared board, and a comfortable and joyful family seated in expectation. If all had not a turkey before them, at least there was the usual substitute—the renowned Christmas goose, which for many appreciative Milesians is sweeter to the tooth than the celebrated American fowl. How many jokes were cracked on the bird and those that ate it! How many little boys of ten or twelve teased their big sisters of fifteen on the slender portion they had received!

It is true that all these details are worse than commonplace; but human life in its happiest moments is made up of such trifles, and the heart expands under the influence of the most ordinary incidents. One thing is certain: that if Christians in Troy were not served with nectar and ambrosia, as they say was served to the gods on Olympus, what they ate and drank was just as pleasing; and, what was still better, there was no after-dinner quarrel among them, such as took place more than once at Jupiter's board, if we must believe Homer himself.

Happening to enter on the evening of that day a house whither I often went to visit the children (for they were more numerous there than elsewhere, though there was, thank God! no lack of them anywhere that I could see), I was highly gratified by the sight of a Christmas-tree. This laudable custom has come to us from Germany, I think. It was not often that the same could be seen in my parish, because, I suppose, it is not a custom of Tipperary. What a *tableau vivant* I had then under my eyes! Fifteen *children* from three years of age to twenty-two, all in a circle around a fine spruce sapling loaded with bundles of every description! Father and mother, of course, distributed the prizes; and if some unlucky chance excited in the heart of the recipient a feeling of disappointment at the oddity of a gift, that was only the more amusing for the fourteen other children, and caused them to laugh boisterously and jump and clap their hands. Just after I had entered and taken my seat the biggest boy (of twenty-two) received for his share a great boot made of pasteboard that dangled from the very top of the tree, and everybody looked eagerly to know what this mysterious boot contained. I shall not enumerate everything, as the list would be too long. The misfortune was that this list was composed mainly of parcels all alike—that is to say, of sheets of brown paper perfectly empty when they were unfolded, and the disconsolate youth of twenty-two had to unfold fifty of them at least before he came to the last, which contained just a small stick of candy of the size of my finger. What a hurrah followed this discovery!

Such were the simple delights of the people. But our main object is to describe the pleasures of birds, and we have not, as it were, even touched the subject. Had the Twit-Twats their Christmas day? Yes! I have said that at that time they invariably enjoy their *winter festival*, which may be considered as a Christmas for birds, who have no soul to save, no sins to deplore, and no virtues to practise.

And to be exact on the subject—for astronomy and theology are concerned in it—I must state precisely what are the ideas and practices of the Twit-Twats in so important a matter. In the evolutionary process which goes on constantly for them, as for everything else, if we must believe Mr. Darwin, they have not yet reached the exact calculations by which man has ascertained the precise recurrence of Christmas. It is well known that among us all movable feasts depend on Easter Sunday, and it has taken us centuries of learned researches to come to a reliable conclusion. The sparrows, always wise in their instinctive appreciation of things in general, have thought that they could dispense with the extraordinary labor undertaken by man to reach a true astronomical result on the subject. As they are so clumsy in their nest-building, they prudently inferred that it would be foolish on their part to tempt fortune in the construction of optical instruments. Their eyes, which are much keener than ours, suffice for them, and they certainly often look at the sun and the moon and the stars for some definite purpose of their own. With their sight alone they could have calculated the conjunction of planets, which is so important in the question under investigation. But they preferred to rely on man's calculations, which they thought were safe enough for all useful purposes. The great difficulty with the sparrows in the present case was that their ideas of *time* are not so precise as ours, although they undoubtedly know to a certain extent what time is. Yet it is doubtful if they have reached the notions of minutes and seconds; nay, we would not dogmatically decide that they have a precise idea of hours. The days even, to consider the question fairly, depend for them more on the weather than on the invariable circle of twenty-four hours. And this last consideration is of such extreme importance that we shall presently come back to it.

They certainly decided among themselves that their *winter festival* should be celebrated on the day appointed for Christmas among us. For the happy recurrence of that great epoch for man had not escaped their observation. It was to be hoped that, since everything is instinctive among them, and instinct usually acts as regularly as clock-work, there would always be an exact correspondence between their great period of winter enjoyment and song (such as we are soon going to describe) and our own *festivitas festivitatum*, which constantly falls on the 25th of December. Unfortunately, what has just been said of their indistinct notion of time becomes often a fatal cause of disagreement between them and ourselves. It has been justly remarked that they judge of time almost altogether by the state of the weather, and this sadly interferes with their calendar.

But have they, in fact, a calendar at all? It is probable they have not, either written or unwritten. If they had, and rain should happen to pour down on a day marked in their almanac as a feast of uncommonly high degree, they would do as men invariably do, and rest and gambol and play in the most unpropitious weather. But they never think of being so foolish. They have only one resource left in such a case —they postpone their festival until the first bright day. In this they are wise, though they show themselves to be very poor astronomers. This was the first point announced a few paragraphs back; sparrow astronomy was the first consideration.

Are they better theologians? A word must suffice on this mighty question. In very truth, this has already been decided, for it has been said with justice that "they have no soul to save, no sins to deplore, no virtues to practise." There are, however, some qualifications to this pregnant phrase which must detain us for a moment. They are certainly creatures of God; their Maker has imposed upon them laws which they sacredly respect and obey. Since they have "no sins to deplore," they are in one sense more acceptable to God than those monstrous sinners who continue to prevaricate as long as they live, and leap into eternity without a sigh of repentance or a single cry for mercy. But there is much more than this. Read the Psalms of holy David, and the songs of the three children in the fiery furnace:

"O ye fountains, bless the Lord; . . . O ye seas and rivers, bless the Lord; . . . O ye whales, . . . bless the Lord; . . . O all ye FOWLS of the air, bless the Lord; praise and exalt Him above all for ever."

The sparrows themselves, consequently, are invited by the Holy Ghost himself—the true inspirer of David and Daniel—"to bless the Lord, to praise and exalt Him above all for ever." Will anybody accuse me after this of gross anthropomorphism—nay, of idolatry, and perhaps fetichism—if I tell my readers that in the great winter festival which I am going to describe the Twit-Twats actually "blessed the Lord, and praised and exalted Him above all for ever"? They were, therefore, to a certain extent, good theologians.

The last preliminary to this description so often announced, and evidently so impatiently expected, will consist in the remark that for this year of 187- the winter festival of the sparrows coincided exactly with the Christian's Christmas day. As the weather was all that could be desired, the Twit-Twats were not reduced to the sad necessity of postponing it, but early in the morning, when the people were still in church, as has been seen, they began their gambols; but particularly in the afternoon, when Trojan Christians were relishing their Christmas dinner, all the trees in the avenues and streets of the city, above all the renowned Lombardy poplars near the St. Joseph's rectory, and the vines and creepers of the friendly convent, were literally swarming with peaceful armies of sparrows, among whom the Twit-Twats were first and foremost in the whole number.

As to the morning, they were rather lazy. They unfortunately do not pay much attention to bells, and all the chimes in the city and the suburbs could not bring them out of their holes. But when the first High Mass was nearly finished, and the organists in the various Catholic churches were still going on with Lambilotte's Christmas Pastoral, so lively and dramatic, the sun at last peacefully arose in the east, shorn of its rays, it is true, and still immersed in the thick vapors of Tethys' aquatic kingdom—the reader must forgive this mythological reminiscence. True enough, however, it was the sun, and the sparrows' instinct could not be deceived. Out they came from their deep sleep, and began to stir themselves about to show that they were alive. They at once thought of their *festival*, and saw with pleasure that there was no need of a postponement. They set at it right away, and as the people were leaving the churches the sparrows were to be seen and heard wherever you went.

To be sure they were not yet firing their big guns. For it is to be remarked that in their great *social* displays they follow the example of the French in their most solemn *national* celebrations. I used often to remark this in France when I was a boy. In the forenoon of those great days of *la St. Louis* under the Bourbons, *la St. Napoléon* under the Empire, or *la Ste. République* the remainder of the time, there was in the morning absolutely nothing of consequence save the firing of cannons by the military, which nobody went to see except old bummers or young *gamins*. But in the afternoon and evening all sorts of amusements were crowded together—rope-walking by acrobats, climbing the greasy pole for sailors and slaters, music by the band of the regiment, regattas on the Loire, races on foot and on horseback, feats of magic by jugglers, Punch and Judy in the open air, grand-style comedy *à la Place Graslin*, and finally great displays of fireworks after sunset.

This usual French programme the Twit-Twats carried through in their winter festivals to the letter; the morning affair was intended only to whet the appetite. Their mock fight with artillery was also after the French model. Not that they used columbiads or thirty-six and twenty-four pounders. The noise came from their throats only, and consequently could not even stun you. It would better express it, perhaps, to say that it somewhat resembled the explosion of small crackers such as little boys and girls use in this happy country every 4th of July morning, when the City Council does not forbid it by ordinance. But it was far from being so annoying; so that there is no fear that the Mayor and Aldermen of New York will ever think of abolishing the sparrow custom. Not only this, but the people who were returning home from Mass seemed to like it very much, and on one occasion I saw a troop of women stop in their walk to look up at the sparrows, and I heard one of them say to one of the sparrows: "Cheer up, little birdy, and keep up your spirits till this afternoon."

The afternoon, in fact, was to give me a sample of a genuine birds' *winter festival* such as I have often witnessed in this country.

This extraordinary display is often seen in the sparrows' republic whenever a few days of mild weather intervene in the cold months of the year. But when this happens exactly on the 25th of December it is accompanied with uncommon splendor and infallibly surprises the beholder. And let not the reader suppose there is any fiction in all this. It can be witnessed by any one who chooses to pay attention to it almost any day that the air is soft and the atmosphere pleasant during our long winters; and it can be particularly studied at leisure in the quiet suburbs of those cities where the birds have permanently established their quarters. It is in circumstances of this kind that I have myself been often struck by it; but it was always in the early part of the afternoon that I observed it, and the sun was invariably shining gently and mildly at the time. Shortly before sunset the birds' activity is still greater than at any other part of the day, and everything is then seen to the best advantage.

On the great occasion which now deserves all our attention I was looking for something better than usual, but was far from anticipating what I was really to witness. After our Christmas dinner, upon going to my room and opening the door, I perceived through both my windows a great agitation in the Lombardy poplars in front. The trees were, of course, quite bare, yet looked as if miraculously covered with foliage, and at the same time as if their hanging leaves were all rocking under the sway of a gentle wind. I ran at once to one of the windows without opening it, and judge of my surprise at what I saw.

What I first took to be poplar-leaves were nothing less than a multitude of my dear Twit-Twats. They literally covered all the branches and the smallest twigs of the trees. They occupied every possible position that a sparrow can take, but the position of each was constantly shifting, as if it had been absolutely impossible for them to remain a moment quiet. I confess that I never witnessed such an extraordinary agility displayed by any acrobat. It is true I was not lucky enough to see the celebrated Blondin's feats, but I think I have looked on his equal more than once. Did I not once see a bold fellow, perched on a rope just sixty feet from the ground, suddenly jump through a paper balloon, and, as everybody thought he would fall and dash out his brains on the pavement below, catch the rope he had just left and appear again in his former proud position? But it was nothing to many of my sparrows' pranks.

And mind that when you are admiring an acrobat he is alone, or perhaps he is accompanied by a couple of poor fellows like himself, and the three together are lost in space at a height of nearly one hundred feet above your head. But in each of the Lombardy poplars there were hundreds of acrobats, all dancing and jumping and flying about, and returning to their former perch, resting on one foot or on both, as you liked best. For they appeared to consult your wishes; and when you said to yourself, How I should like to see this or that! it immediately happened as you had desired.

Now, to render this spectacle more interesting the sun was shining as brightly as it ever can in December, and its rays, already declining toward the west, were gently touching the glass of my windows after having passed through the maze of the playing birds. It was a pleasure to look at these *freaks of light*. Having been used long, long ago to study optics, and catoptrics, and dioptrics, and all that, I could easily follow the action of the laws of nature as to the diffusion, refraction, reflection, and decomposition of light into its primitive colors. After a few moments' attention I could distinguish as many small rainbows as there were spaces between the sparrows and the trees, and without a glass prism at all I had under my eyes as many prismatic colors as I could wish.

The material laws of the world, therefore, were combining together with the social laws guiding sparrows and men to render this *winter festival* complete in all respects. Nature had taken her best attire and decked herself with all her finery to help the gentle Twit-Twats " to bless the Lord and praise Him above all for ever."

And, to complete the happy combination of all things toward the same object, there was music also, but not the music of trumpets and clarions. The harmony was far sweeter than that, and it deserves a particular description, which I think I am warranted to give, for (to speak scientifically) I have made a particular study of every kind of sparrow counterpoint.

I think I have already spoken of their screams when fighting and pursuing each other in the summer or the spring-time; but this can scarcely be called music. I may have mentioned also the frank and open baritone voice with which the individuals of each couple answer one another from two different and often distant branches. But in their winter festivals they do not use such primitive music as that. The same may almost be said of the gentler songs they usually employ in their private colloquies, when they are near each other, in small groups of three or four, and they speak in singing tones (for their language is always more or less musical). Even then the softness of the melody cannot compare with what is heard, for instance, in the afternoon of the 25th of every December. A word has likewise been said a few paragraphs back of the more harmonious strain issuing from their throats at early morning, when they first awake and the trees are alive with dancing birds and resound with their twitter. It has been said with justice that their music at that particular moment somewhat resembles the incessant explosions of fire-crackers early in the morning of the Fourth of July. But even this cannot in the least be compared to the soft warbling of their winter festivals, for this last is far more subdued and it blends in real harmony. You would imagine that hundreds and hundreds of Æolian harps suspended in the air were at the same instant receiving the softest touch of the gentlest of zephyrs. Nor ought any one suppose that the bands of military music which I have often heard in Nantes in my native France on great national celebrations could enchant me as much as the harmony I was privileged to listen to in Troy at the great Christmas festival of 187-.

As to climbing the greasy pole, the regattas, the races on foot and on horseback, the feats of magic, the tragical drama of Punch and Judy, and the grand-style *comédies bourgeoises* usual in France on great occasions, it might be easily proved that the Twit-Twats either enjoyed the best features of all these entertainments or had some amusements of a far higher order to compensate for the absence of any of them. The only thing they lacked was fireworks, for which they had no fancy, as they were invariably asleep in their holes at the time when fireworks should be displayed.

After having witnessed from my room so delightful a sight as I have described, I determined to find out if anything similar was going on in places beyond the reach of vision from my windows. It had been wisely arranged that the grand Vespers in the church should for that day be sung in the evening at half-past six. This would give time to all the parishioners to protract their dinners till late in the afternoon, if they chose. I had, therefore, leisure to pursue my researches, and from my house I went straight to the convent and its neighborhood, thence along Fourth Street as far as the bridge over Poestenkill Creek, and then, crossing over to Third and First Streets, I knew that I should find plenty of trees along those thoroughfares, which would give me a grand opportunity of ascertaining a matter of so great interest to me.

What I saw at all points gratified me beyond expression. First, every human being happening to be then at his dinner or engaged in conversation with his friends, there was the greatest stillness and peace on all sides. It looked as if that part of the city had been suddenly transformed into a solitude. No wagons or cars in the streets; no urchins to distract you on the way; neither were there gloomy pedestrians nor boisterous groups with their jokes and laughter. The Twit-Twats had the whole district to themselves, and they knew, the little rogues, how to improve their opportunity. The splendid feats of rope-dancing that had enchanted me under my windows were going on in all directions as far as you could see. But I found with surprise and pleasure that the best exploits of that kind were performed along the Creek, where there were no trees of any kind. A great number of telegraph poles and wires were in that neighborhood, whilst there was not a single wire near my house. I am sure that the sparrows imagined, innocent souls! that the posts had been planted in the ground and the wires stretched across lots and river only for their own special benefit. Troops of sparrows were either perched on the wires, resting for a moment, or hanging from them in trapeze style and describing every sort of curve. Blondin or any other *acrobat*, as I think I called him, could not have competed with them in that healthful exercise.

As to the music, it was everywhere a repetition of what I had heard from the rectory. I have spoken of hundreds of Æolian harps; I found in my rambles that it would be more exact to speak of thousands of them. But the quality of the melody was everywhere the same. Our great composers, in order, with their usual systems of notation, to express this music, would have to employ exclusively those signs which mark the nearly inaudible whispers, the sighs and hushed sounds by which they generally express the fall of the dew, the movement of light, and the silence that follows thunder!

There is no exaggeration here. Whoever has been present at one of the sparrows' great winter festivals must agree that it is true, and that their music on these occasions is peculiar to these, and is never employed by the birds for any other object. As we say that with us a melancholy song must be written in a minor key, so of the sparrows it must be maintained that for winter festivals nothing can be used in the composition except whispers and sighs, intermixed with silence. It is something like what you hear on the sea-shore when the still waters of the ocean ebb slowly away, and sing a dreamy ditty by playing on the diminutive shells of the beach.

How could so happy a day pass off so rapidly? For the end of it soon came, and memory alone could call it back. But at least the profound peace which had distinguished it remained.

Every cause of alarm was removed by the complete disappearance of the boisterous native birds, who were never heard of afterwards. The Twit-Twat empire was surely to last for a long period at least, since nothing here below is eternal; and its annals since could all be comprised in a few insignificant phrases, as is usual with the history of all happy nations. The great Christmas day of 187- inaugurated this era of peace, and must on this account remain for ever enshrined in my memory.

But it is not that day alone which continues dear and sweet in my remembrance. The reader can easily imagine that the whole year occupied in my observations and reflections was a period of entrancing enjoyment and happiness. It was about that time that I received occasional visits from a Protestant lady who had placed herself under my direction and instruction to be admitted into the Church. On one occasion she expressed a kind of sorrow that my lot was cast in the midst of poor people living by hard labor, unrefined, and incapable, she thought, of casting any glow of poetry over my life among them.

"You mistake, madam," I replied; "and this remark comes, I suppose, rather from what you have heard than from your own feelings. On the point of becoming a child of the true Church, you know that the salvation of souls is more important and delightful than poetry; and I assure you that in this very place there is for a Christian pastor an infinite delight in leading to heaven pure, though perhaps unrefined, souls, full of gratitude for what is done for them, and so easy to lead that there is scarcely ever any difficulty in our ministry. But besides this interior world of the Christian spirit, which is as full—if not fuller—of beauty, in the midst of such a people as live around me as among the most educated and refined, there is, I tell you, true poetry on all sides. The only thing needed is to know how to discern and find it. Why, madam, in this poor spot, as you imagine, there is rather too much of it, and for conscience' sake I have often to turn away my eyes from this exterior glitter and fall back on more solid food, which I feel I need to fulfil my strict duty as a Catholic priest. To obey Christ's injunction we must be the 'salt of the earth'; and of all the materials of which the earth is composed salt is perhaps the least poetical and calculated to excite the imagination. We are not denied, however, the right of making a proper use of that faculty, and in this our advantage is as great at least as that of any other man, whatever may be his ability. Our holy religion is a perpetual well-spring of the purest, highest, and holiest imagination; and on this account alone, not taking the solid part of our ministry into account, I would not exchange my place with that of Mr. Beecher, who may be surrounded by crowds of fashionable people, and receives from them, I hear, twenty-five thousand dollars a year for his *salary!* I do not receive from my parishioners, thank Heaven! any other salary than their affection; but I expect my reward from God."

This little speech appeared to produce a deep impression on the good lady to whom it was addressed, and soon after she entered the Church.

www.ingramcontent.com/pod-product-compliance
Lightning Source LLC
Chambersburg PA
CBHW020159170426
43199CB00010B/1105